I0090156

The Change¹⁹

Insights into Self-Empowerment

Jim Britt ~ Jim Lutes

With

Co-authors From Around the World

The Change[19]

Jim Britt ~ Jim Lutes

All Rights Reserved

Copyright 2022

The Change

10556 Combie Road, Suite 6205

Auburn, CA 95602

The use of any part of this publication, whether reproduced, stored in any retrieval system or transmitted in any forms or by any means, electronic or otherwise, without the prior written consent of the publisher, is an infringement of copyright law.

Jim Lutes ~ Jim Britt

The Change

ISBN#

Co-authors

Jim Britt

Jim Lutes

Dr. Elizabeth Ssemanda

Rachel Best

Christian Rhodes

Dr. Karen Kramer

Michael Cupo

Cheryl Elizabeth Williams

Lindsaya VanDeusen

Ira S Wolfe

Nancey Sinclaire

Darcee D. McJannet

Karl E, Fryburg

Dr. Patricia Rogers

Nicole Harvick

Deana Brown Mitchell

Heather Bach

Susan Kennard

Rose Marie Young

Dr. Tianna Conte

Peggy Sealfon

Renu Sethi

iv

DEDICATION

To all those who dedicate their life to helping others live a more
fulfilled life

Foreword

By Les Brown

Many of us spend at least a good part of our day going over internal dialog. We relive past experiences, worry about the future, blame the outside world for our shortcomings and criticize ourselves for not having all we want by this point in our lives. We do this both consciously and unconsciously. Even while we are listening to others, we aren't really fully present. Instead, we are rehearsing our answers, slipping back into yesterday and worrying about tomorrow.

We live in uncertain times. We all feel we have minimum control over being able to change external circumstances, but we do have control over being able to change our internal environment, not only being able to see the truth behind a given situation but also how we respond to it. And to get the best out of the most stressful times, we need to demand the best from ourselves.

Many feel the pain of unhappiness. So many suffer from it daily, unaware that they can eliminate their suffering and find happiness by simply seeing the truth behind their unhappiness and making the right choices to change it. The problem is that our emotional conflicts are so familiar to us that they keep us blinded to better possibilities. We actually become addicted to feeling the way we do, thinking that it is just the way things are and we resign ourselves to getting by and coping.

I have had the privilege of speaking for over forty years serving millions of people from over 51 different countries. I know that there are certain patterns that create success and other patterns that breed internal conflict and failures.

The secret to being fulfilled and living the life you want is having the courage to go beyond the skills you've learned and discover the gifts that you were born with and to implement them daily. So many people settle for less in life, but I can tell you from my experience that it doesn't have to be that way.

I was born in an abandoned building on a floor with a twin brother in a poor section in Miami Florida called Liberty City. When we were six weeks of age, we were adopted by Mrs. Mimi Brown.

Whenever I speak, I always say that all that I am and all I ever hope to be I owe to my mother.

When I was in the fifth grade, I was labeled educable mentally retarded and put back from the fifth grade to the fourth grade and failed again when I was in the eighth grade. Mrs. Mimi Brown took my brother and I and five other kids in as foster kids and eventually adopted us.

Because of the work that Jim Britt does and the methods and techniques he uses to change your story and how you see yourself, it enabled me to build my career to make it against all odds. Both Jim Britt and Jim Lutes are icons in personal development and empowering others to be the best they can be.

You have something special inside. You have greatness in you. When you read this book it will take you on a journey and introduce you to a part of yourself that has remained hidden and you didn't know existed.

When you begin to look at your goals and dreams realize that you have greatness inside you. The Change will provide the insights and processes of self-development that will empower you to manifest your greatness.

Jim Britt and I actually started the foundation of our speaking careers in the same direct selling company, Bestline, over 40 years ago. Although I haven't followed Jim Britt's career over the years, but I do know that he is recognized as one of the top thought leaders in the world, helping millions of people create prosperous lives, rewarding relationships and spiritual awareness. He has authored 13 books and multiple programs showing people how to understand their hidden abilities to do more, become more and enjoy more in every area of life.

Today, Jim Britt and mind programming expert, Jim Lutes, along with inspiring co-authors from around the world, bring a pioneering work "The Change" book series to the market to transform lives. Their principles are forged on touching millions on every continent. As you read, you are exploring self-empowerment principles from a whole different perspective. In fact, Jim and Jim's publications of The Change book series now has hundreds of coauthors in 26 countries. The real power in each book is that 20 coauthors share their inspiring story so that the reader may benefit from their experience. It is packed with life-changing ideas, stories, tips, strategies on various empowering topics that you will love.

The principles, concepts and ideas within this book are sometimes simple, but can be profound to a person who is ready for that perfect message at the right time and is willing to take action to change. Maybe for one it's a chapter on relationships or leadership. For the next maybe it's a chapter on forgiveness or health awareness, and for another a simple life-changing message like I received as a youngster from a teacher. Each chapter is like opening a surprise empowering gift.

As I travel the world presenting my seminars, I meet people who spend more time and energy focused on what's wrong with society and their lives than is spent on helping each other improve the quality of life. With so much time spent on social media we often fear intimate contact with each other. Mistrust is often our first reaction. We judge and sometimes brutalize those among us who are in any way different from ourselves. We become addicted to anything that allows us a brief consolidation from the terrible pain we feel inside.

We need to begin to understand more about ourselves and our condition if there is ever to be the possibility of a healthy society. I believe this is possible and that's why I am so passionate about the work I do. Simply put…we are at war with ourselves. Real healing only takes place when we are willing to experience and face the truth within.

The conclusion to me is an exciting one. You, me and every other human being are shaping our brains and bodies by the thoughts we think, the emotions we feel, the intentions we hold, and the actions we take daily. Why is it exciting? Because we are in control of all these things and we can change as long as we have the intention, willingness and commitment to look inside, take charge of our lives and make the changes.

Whether you're pursuing, your dreams as an entrepreneur, a business owner or you want a more fulfilling relationship, or simply want to live a happy life, being authentic and actively appreciating what you're really capable of is going to be one of the most important assets you possess. It will make the difference between just "getting by" and really thriving and experiencing happiness or internal conflict.

Self-knowledge provides you the emotional edge that will help you create a better life not only for yourself, but also for everyone with whom you come in contact.

This is the time to extract the best out of yourself and to use that gift to touch the lives of others.

I want to congratulate Jim Britt and Jim Lutes for making this publication series available and for allowing me to write the foreword. I honor them both and the coauthors within this book and the series for the lives they are changing.

As you enter these pages, do so slowly and with an open mind. Savor the wisdom you discover here, and then with interest and curiosity discover what rings true for you, and then take action toward the life you want.

Be prepared…because your life is about to change.

Hope to meet you one day at one of my seminars. And remember, everything you do counts!

Les Brown

Table of Contents

Jim Britt

Jim Britt is an award-winning author of 15 best-selling books and nine #1 International best-sellers. Some of his many titles include Rings of Truth, Do This. Get Rich-For Entrepreneurs, Unleashing Your Authentic Power, The Power of Letting Go, Cracking the Rich Code and The Entrepreneur.

He is an internationally recognized business and life strategist who is highly sought after as a keynote speaker, both online and live, for all audiences.

As an entrepreneur Jim has launched 28 successful business ventures. He has served as a success strategist to over 300 corporations worldwide and was recently named as one of the world's top 50 speakers and top 20 success coaches. He was presented with the "Best of the Best" award out of the top 100 contributors of all time to the Direct Selling industry.

For over four decades Jim has presented seminars throughout the world sharing his success strategies and life enhancing realizations with over 5,000 audiences, totaling almost 2,000,000 people from all walks of life.

Early in his speaking career he was Business partners with the late Jim Rohn for eight years, where Tony Robbins worked under Jim's direction for his first few years in the speaking business.

As a performance strategist, Jim leverages his skills and experience as one of the leading experts in peak performance, entrepreneurship and personal empowerment to produce stellar results. He is pleased to work with small business entrepreneurs, and anyone seeking to remove the blocks that stop their success in any area of their life.

One of Jim's latest programs "Cracking the Rich Code" focuses on the subconscious programs influencing one's relationship with money and their financial success.

www.CrackingTheRichCode.com

Think Like Superman

By Jim Britt

"Waking up to your true greatness in life requires letting go of who you imagine yourself to be."

--- Jim Britt

FACT: Becoming a millionaire is easier than it has ever been.

Many people have the notion that it's an impossible task to become a millionaire. Some say, "It's pure luck." Others say, "You have to be born into a rich family." For others, "You'll have to win the Lotto." And for many they say, "Your parents have to help you out a lot." That's the language of the poor.

A single mother with five children says, "I want to believe in what you're saying. However, I'm 45 years old and work long hours at two dead-end jobs. I barely earn enough to get by. What should I do?"

Another man said, "Well, if you work for the government, you cannot expect to become a millionaire. After all, you're on a fixed salary and there's little time for anything else. By the time you get home, you've got to play with the kids, eat dinner, and fall asleep watching TV."

Everyone has a story as to why they could never become a millionaire. But for every story, excuse really, there are other stories OR PEOPLE with worse circumstances, that have become rich.

The truth is that all of us can become as wealthy as we decide to be, and that's a mindset. None of us is excluded from wealth. If you have the desire to receive money, whatever the amount, you have all of the rights to do so like everyone else. There is no limit to how much you can earn for yourself. The only limitations are what you place on yourself.

Money is like the sun. It does not discriminate. It doesn't say, "I will not give light and warmth to this flower, tree, or person because I don't like them." Like the sun, money is abundantly available to all of us who truly believe that it is for us. No one is excluded.

There are, however, some major differences between rich and poor people. Here are some tips for becoming rich.

Change Your Thinking

You have to see the bigger picture. There are opportunities everywhere! The problem is that most people see just trees, when they should be looking at the entire forest. By doing so you will see that there are opportunities everywhere. The possibilities are endless.

You'll also have to go through plenty of <u>self-discovery</u> before you earn your first million. Knowing the truth about yourself isn't always the easiest task. Sometimes, you'll find that you are your biggest enemy—at least some days.

Learn from Millionaires

Most people are surrounded by what I like to call their, "default friends." These friends are acquaintances that we see at the gym, school, work, local happy hour, and other places. We naturally befriend these people because we are all in the same boat financially. However, in most cases, these people aren't millionaires and cannot help you become one either. In fact, if you tell them you are going to become a millionaire, some may even tell you that it's impossible and discourage you from even trying. They'll tell you that you're living in a fantasy world and why you'll never be able to make it happen. Instead, learn from millionaires. Let go of these relationships that pull you down when it comes to your money desires. It's okay to have friends that aren't millionaires. However, only take input from those that have accomplished what you want to accomplish. Hang out with those that will encourage and help you get to the next level. Don't give your raw diamonds to a brick layer to be cut.

Indulge in Wealth

To become wealthy, you must learn about wealth. This means that you'll have to put yourself in situations that you've never been in before.

ON OCCASION, DO SOME OF THESE:

Fly first class and see how it makes you feel.

Eat out at the finest restaurant and don't look at the price.

Take a limo instead of a cab or Uber. Watch how you feel.

Reserve a suite in a first-class hotel.

If you are used to drinking a $20 bottle of wine, go for the $100 and see how it tastes. It does taste different.

All I am saying is, try some of the things that wealthy people do and see how it makes you feel.

Believe it is Possible

If you believe that it is possible to become a millionaire, you can make it happen. However, if you've excluded yourself from this possibility and think and believe that it's for other people, you'll never become a millionaire.

Also, be sure to bless rich people when you can. Haters of money aren't likely to receive any of it either.

Read books that have been written by millionaires. By gaining a well-rounded education about earning large sums of money and staying inspired, you'll be able to learn the wealth secrets of the rich. I just saw a video on LinkedIn with my friend Kevin Harrington from the TV show Shark Tank. He said that one of his new companies just had a million-dollar day on Amazon.

Enlarge Your Service

Your material wealth is the sum of your total contribution to society. Your daily mantra should be, *'How do I deliver more value to more people in less time?'* Then, you'll know that you can always increase your quality and quantity of service. Enlarging your service is also about going the extra mile. When it comes to helping others, you must give it everything you have. You just plant the seeds and nature will take care of the rest.

Seize ALL Opportunities That Make Sense

You cannot say "No" to opportunities and expect to become a millionaire. You must seize every opportunity that has your name on it. It may just be an opportunity to connect with an influential person for no reason. Sometimes the monetary reward will not come immediately, but if you keep planting seeds, eventually you'll grow a fruitful crop. Money is the harvest of the service you provide and sometimes the connections you have. The more seeds you plant, the greater the harvest.

Have an Unstoppable Mindset

Want to know some of what my first mentor shared with me that took me from a broke factory worker, high school dropout, to millionaire?

First, he said, you have to start thinking like a wealthy, unstoppable person. You have to have a wealth mindset. He said that wealthy people think differently. He said, "I want you to start thinking like Superman!" Sounds crazy, right? Well, it's not. It's powerful and here's why. How you think will change your life.

Wealthy people think differently. They really do. And anyone can learn to think like the wealthy.

I'm not talking about positive thinking, Law of Attraction, or motivation. Let's get real. None of that stuff works anyway. Otherwise, we would all be rich and happy already. I'm talking about thinking based in quantum physics science. Once you understand and apply it, it will change your life. You will become unstoppable!

If there was any person, fictional or real, whose qualities you could instantly possess, who would that person be? Think about it. Personally, I would say that Superman is the perfect person. Now, you are probably thinking I have lost it right? Just stick with me here. I think you will like what you are about to hear.

Superman is a fictional superhero widely considered to be one of the most famous and popular action hero and an American cultural icon. I remember watching Superman every Saturday morning when I was a kid. I couldn't get enough. He was my hero!

Let's look at Superman's traits:

Superman is indestructible.

He is a man of steel.

He can stop a locomotive in its tracks.

Bullets bounce off him.

He is faster than a speeding bullet.

No one can bring him down.

He can leap tall buildings in a single bound. Great powers to have in this day-and-age, wouldn't you say? What else would you need?

Now, for all you females, don't worry, we have not left you out. There is also a female version of Superman, named Superwoman. She has the same powers as Superman.

Now, this is where it gets interesting. Let's first look at the qualities that Superman possesses that you want to make your own. And to make it simple, I will refer to Superman for the rest of this message, and you can replace with Superwoman if you are female.

Again:

Superman is powerful and fearless.

Superman is virtually indestructible—except for kryptonite of course.

Superman can stop bullets.

Superman has supernatural powers. He can see through walls.

Superman can stop a speeding locomotive.

Superman can stop a bullet.

Superman jumps into immediate action when troubles arise.

Superman can crash through barriers.

Superman can even change clothes in a phone booth in seconds. Not too many of those around anymore. You'll have to duck behind a building to change.

So, you're thinking right now, *'Ok, I know that Superman has incredible supernatural powers, how can that help me? What good will it do me to think I am Superman, a fictional character?'*

Here is where science comes in. This is the part where you will be amazed when you learn about the supernatural powers that you already possess! NO, REALLY!

Your brain makes certain chemicals called neuro peptides. These are literally the molecules of emotion, like love, fear, joy, passion, and so on. These molecules of emotion are not only contained in your brain they actually circulate throughout your cellular structure. They send out a signal, a frequency much like a radio station sending out a signal. For example, you tune to 92.5 and you get jazz. Tune to 99.6 and you get rock. And if you are just one decimal off, you get static. The difference is that your signal goes both ways. You are a sender and a receiver.

You put out a signal, a mindset, of confidence about your financial success and people, circumstances, and opportunities show up to support your success. When you put out a signal of doubt and uncertainty and you receive support for your doubt and uncertainty. You've been around someone that you didn't trust, or you felt less than positive just being in their presence, right? You have also been around people that inspire you. That's what I'm talking about. You are projecting a frequency, looking to resonate with the frequency you are transmitting.

Anyway, the amazing part about these cells of emotion is that they are intelligent. They are thinking cells. These cells are constantly eavesdropping on the conversation that you are having with yourself. That's right. They are listening to you! And others are listening to your cells as well. Others feel what you feel when they are around you.

Your unconscious mind, your cells, are listening in, waiting to adjust your behavior based on what they hear from you, their master. So just imagine what would happen if you started to think like Superman...or like a millionaire.

Here are some of the thoughts you might have during the day:

"The challenges I face day today are easily overcome, after all I am Superman."

"I am indestructible."

"I have incredible strength."

"Nothing can stop me.....NOTHING."

"I have supernatural powers and can overcome anything."

"I can accomplish anything I want when I put my mind to it."

"I can break through any barrier."

"I can and I will do whatever it takes to accomplish my goal."

"I fear nothing."

The trillions of thinking cells in your body and brain listen, and they create exactly what you tell them to create. Their mission is to complete the picture of the you they see and hear when you talk to them. They must obey. It's their job!

Since you are Superman, you cannot fail. Why? Your thinking cells are now sending out the right signal, because you told them to. They are making you stronger, more successful, everyday! You have the ability to fight off all negativity, doubt, fear, and worry—nothing can stop you!

Superman has total confidence. So, your cells of emotion relating to confidence will now create more neuro peptide chemicals to promote feelings of power and confidence that others will feel in your presence.

Superman is fearless. So, your cells of emotion relating to fear will now create more neuro peptide chemicals to create feelings of courage. You are unstoppable!

And here's the key. Others will respond to you in the same way that you are talking to yourself.

If you are confident, others will have confidence in you.

You have thousands of thoughts every day. Make sure your thoughts are leading you in the direction you want to go. Make sure you are telling your cells a success story, and not a 'woe is me' story.

Most have been conditioned to think that creating wealth is difficult, or that it's only for the lucky few. What do you believe? It doesn't cost you any more to think like Superman; and it's much more inspiring!

Mediocrity cannot be an option if you decide to be wealthy and think like Superman.

Your decision, and communication with your cells, creates a mindset; that mindset influences how you show up.

None of that old type of thinking matters anymore…after all, you are Superman, and you can accomplish anything.

If you want wealth, you have to stretch yourself. You have to do the things that unsuccessful people are not willing to do. You have to say "yes" to opportunity, then figure out how to get the job done.

Maybe you are uncomfortable selling and asking for money. If that's the case, then learn sales and learn to ask for money every day until you feel comfortable asking for it. You will never have money if you don't learn to ask for it.

I've learned a lot in the past 40+ years as an entrepreneur. I've learned that in order to have more, you have to become more. I've also learned that if you are comfortable, you are not growing. I learned that I couldn't go from a nervous rookie speaker with minimal self-confidence to hosting TV shows and speaking in front of 5,000 people overnight. I simply wasn't ready. I grew into that, one speaking engagement at a time. Every time I finished a speaking engagement, I would ask myself, "How did I do, and how could I do it better?" I still do that today.

And I've learned from the hundreds of thousands of people I've trained, coached, and mentored that none of us can do something we don't believe is possible. It's not going to happen if you're not ready to step out of your comfort zone and stretch yourself.

This has led me to understand the single most important principle of wealth-building, that has meant the difference between poverty and riches for people since humans first traded for pelts.

Are you ready?

Come in just a little closer. Listen up!

Every income level requires a different you, a different mindset! If you think that $10,000 a month is a lot of money, then $100,000 a month will be completely out of reach. If you believe that having $5,000 in the bank would make you rich, then $50,000 won't miraculously appear. You will never earn more money than you believe is "a lot" of money.

What you do as a business is only a small part of becoming rich. In fact, there are thousands, if not tens of thousands, of ways to make money—and lots of it. What I've learned over the years is that, by focusing on who you want to become instead of what you need to do, you're going to multiply your chances of getting rich a hundred-fold.

Ask anyone who's found a way to make a large sum of money legally, and he or she will tell you that it's not hard once you crack the code. And cracking the code starts with you and your mindset. The "code" to which I refer isn't a secret rite or ancient scroll. It's not even a secret. It's a certain way of thinking and believing in which you've trained your mind to see money-making ideas.

That's where you see a need in the marketplace, and you jump on the idea quickly. It might involve creating a new product; or, it may just be teaching others a special technique you've learned. It may even require raising capital to start a company or to market a product or idea on social media.

Don't Hold Back. You Have to Take Action to Change.

Start right now to imagine yourself as already having wealth. How would your life be? How would your day unfold? Start to own your wealth mindset now! The subconscious mind is unable to differentiate between actual fact and mere visualization. So, by imagining that you already have it, you're encouraging your subconscious mind to seek the ways and means to transform your imaginary feelings into the real thing.

Find yourself some mentors. Nobody has all the answers. Surround yourself with people that will support, inspire, and provide you with answers that keep you moving in the right direction. If you truly want to attain wealth, have a thriving business, or reach the top of your game in any endeavor, having a qualified mentor is essential.

Okay, lets come in for a landing …

It is absolutely essential to have a crystal-clear picture of what you want to accomplish before you begin. If you want to attain wealth, you must learn to operate without fear and with a sharply defined mental image of the outcome you want to attain. This comes from thinking like a wealthy person, (like Superman) making decisions like a wealthy person and being fearless (like Superman) when it comes to stepping out of your comfort zone. Look at the end result as something you're already prepared to do, you just haven't done it yet.

Think about this. Your success is something that you have been preventing; it's not something you have to struggle to make happen. The key is to not let fear, doubt, other people, or mind chatter push your success away. You'll find that the solutions taking you toward your goals will come to you in the most unexpected and sudden ways. You don't need the *perfect* plan first. What you need is a perfectly clear decision about your success, the right mindset, the right mentoring, and the ideal way to get you there will materialize.

The greatest transfer of wealth in the history of the human race is happening right now. Are you positioned to get your share?

Remember, in order to get a different result, you must do something different. In order to do something different you must know something different to do. And in order to know something different, you have to first suspect that your present methods need improving.

THEN, YOU HAVE TO BE WILLING TO DO SOMETHING ABOUT IT.

***

For more information on Jim's work:

www.JimBritt.com

http://JimBrittCoaching.com

www.facebook.com/jimbrittonline

www.linkedin.com/in/jim-britt

For free audio series www.RichCode1.com and www.RichCode2.com

http://becomeAcoauthor.com

To find out how to crack the rich code and change your subconscious programming regarding your relationship with money: www.CrackingTheRichCode.com

Jim Lutes

Say the name Jim Lutes and chances are a top performer in your company has attended one or more of his dynamic trainings over the last few years.

Having taught his branded form of human performance since the early 1990s, Mr. Lutes has accelerated top level entrepreneurs throughout his career by conducting trainings on personal growth and subconscious programming into worldwide markets.

During this time Jim took his skills regarding the human mind, and combining it with trainings on influence, persuasion and communication strategies he launched Lutes International in the early 1990s. Based in San Diego California Jim has taught seminars for, corporations, sales forces, individuals and athletes. Having appeared on television, radio and worldwide stages, Jim's style, knowledge and effectiveness provide profound results.

"Jim Lutes possesses a unique ability to create performance change in an individual in a fraction of the time it takes his competitors". The core of human's decisions is based on the programs we acquire, reinforce and grow. Combining Jims various trainings individuals can reach new levels of achievement and fulfillment in all areas of life. The results are at times nothing short of astonishing.

"My goal is to take that embryonic greatness that exists inside every person in America, foster it, empower it and then hand them personal strategies based on solid principles that allow them to take that new attitude and apply it to creating a life masterpiece".

What You do with YOU

By Jim Lutes

Most people think that if they can just learn enough, earn enough, get smart enough, then they will BE enough. And they think that when that happens, they can finally relax and be happy. But what happens is that they get so caught up in what they are constantly *doing* that are not focused on how they are *being.*

In other words, they are not focused on their emotional state. When you engage your emotions you subconscious mind begins to get the messages and begins to establish new rules and new behaviors. And then it becomes a way of life and enters your heart and really begins to come from your heart. When it is in your heart then it is truly part of you. When you are really getting it now at the deepest level, when you can begin to anticipate what I am going to say, you know you understand it at a much deeper level right now.

I began to study human performance as a way to make some changes in my own life and when I began to see some serious results, I got so excited about it that I wanted to share it with other people. And so I committed my life to learning and sharing what works with others. So, I am a committed lifetime learner and therefore I have been fortunate enough to have had the ability to look at and study just about every approach there is to personal development and success that is available in today's market. I am a strong advocate of clear, simple, workable approaches that get dependable and lasting results.

Because of the vast wealth of information my Life Masterpiece teaching gives you and the amazing results you will get, you will likely find yourself returning to it again and again throughout your life.

No matter how successful we are, or how successful we become, we all need a coach to encourage us, to challenge us, to remind us to live up to our potential. I am going to be here to do that for you each day, and it is both my honor and my privilege to serve you in that way.

Let's get started now.

That person that you are and that person that you must become in order to put the colors of your life masterpiece where you want them and blend them in just the right combination to create your own unique experience might right now seem like two very different people, but they are one in the same. You are that person right now. I am going to help you uncover your true identity and purpose so that you can then activate the universal laws and make them work for you.

When we let go of all the stories, we have been telling ourselves about who we think we are supposed to be and what we think we are supposed to do and have, we not only free ourselves we free our families, our children, our intimate partners, and our friends in the process. There is no way you can make a difference in yourself without touching somebody else even if it is not your intention.

The Life Masterpiece focus is about what you can do with YOU. If you want to change any circumstance, any relationship, then you must begin with yourself no matter how convinced you are that somebody else or something else must change. Changing yourself can change even the most rigid system and stubborn person. And ANY progress moves you forward. And any movement forward on your part creates the opportunity for every other part of your life to be moved forward as well.

One of the most effective ways for you to reprogram your mind is through what I like to call vicarious experiences. These are the experiences other people have had and I will bring you through their experiences by sharing their stories with you. These stories are not in this book simply to fill it up and make it fat like you find in some books. These stories are the heart and soul of the book because this is how you will begin to reprogram your subconscious and take the information into your heart where it will transform you.

The reason why vicarious experiences are so powerful is because they relate to you and so when you are reading these stories your conscious mind will get go and your unconscious mind will get the lesson.

And when you read some of these remarkable stories and meet some of these people who have gone through some amazing personal transformations, you will begin to realize that no matter who you are, no matter what part of the world you are from or what culture you grew up in, whether you grow up poor, wealthy or somewhere in between, whether you grow up with religion or Monday Night Football, you will begin to realize that we all have the same problems.

So what will happen is you will begin to connect with these people because they have the same problems you have- the same challenges. They are universal. And you will learn what the reason is for this is that we all have the same basic needs, and our lives are about meeting these needs and that they impact and determine every single thing we do and every decision we make. Every single habit, behavior, rule or pattern is your unconscious way of trying to get your needs met. And your needs are the same exact needs every other human being on the planet has. We all use different behaviors to get these needs met but they are still the same.

Some of the behaviors we use are positive and healthy and some of them are not quite so resourceful. And this is one of the reasons why even though we all have the same needs and the same problems, we all get different results. We are hard wired with the same needs, but not with the same subconscious programming. And the reason why we all get different results boils down to one thing- standards.

You know, so often in life, we find ourselves in a position where we live life a certain way. We act a certain way. We were raised in a certain way. And through our lives in an effort to avoid pain and still meet our needs, we made critical decisions about who we are and how we think we need to be. And so we believe we know who we are.

But the way we have behaved for years is simply an *adaptation*. Something that happened in response to the desire we had to meet our basic needs- to get the love, or respect, or acceptance from a parent, lover, loved one or peers- caused us to make a key decision and adapt to the circumstances around us. We do not ever realize that for years we have been living something that we are really good at but which is not necessarily our true nature.

One of the things you will learn here is that a single decision has the power to change everything in a heartbeat. In fact, when you stay with me through this you are going to learn about a decision, he made perhaps some time ago that his determine the choices you have made in the course of your life up until now. Today he made a decision to pick up this book and begin this journey with me and if you will indulge me for just a few hours the decision to pick up this book might be the decision that changes everything in your life from today on.

Now that you've made the decision to read it, I will tell you what this book can really do for you. It will get you to uncover and maybe for the first time really identify how the role models of your life have affected your subconscious decision-making in ways you never dreamed possible.

Without getting into the actual science behind it, a child's brain works much differently than an adult brain. As you might already know our brains operate using four different wavelengths -- alpha, beta, theta and Delta. Most of the time, the adult brain operates at the beta level when we are awake. The beta level is when our eyes are focused in our conscious mind is in control, and we are logical. The alpha level is a level that we must pass through to go to sleep and to wake up, and it's also the most common level is one we are in a trance. Theta is for a deeper trance or dreaming, and Delta is for deep sleep. This means that when we are at the alpha level, we are highly impressionable, because the messages are going directly into our subconscious minds. A child's mind is different because it operates primarily at the alpha level, which is why children are so impressionable. This also means that our parents and other significant people in our childhood had a tremendous impact on the messages that are subconscious mind received and events from our childhood had a strong impact on our self-image, our identity and how we develop as adults. This is why when we speak about reprogramming the subconscious mind is very important to talk about her childhood and her relationship with her parents. This is not done to point fingers or place blame, but to help us understand some of the reasons for the choices that we make for the patterns that we keep repeating and how they carry over from generation to generation.

Even if you feel like you held your own when you were growing up, and that the relationships that you had as a child -- especially the relationship she had with your mother and father -- were strong, and you feel like you are strong as a result. There are still patterns that your subconscious mind is running that no longer serve you. Because it's the tension, the experience of having to deal with all of the events of your past and even the events that happened before you were born in your parent's past -- all of these experiences affect your decision making, your relationships, your finances, your choices, behaviors and life circumstances, even today.

Even if your childhood was perfect and you feel like you honor, respect and love your parents and adore all of your siblings and even if your parents or your greatest role models, you are still affected on many levels and in many ways. And because you decided to read this book, I believe you have some things you would like to change. If you change anything, first you must learn to reprogram your subconscious mind and part of doing so is to understand that the key decisions you made in the past still impact you today.

Our childhood role models deeply affect both our conscious and subconscious decision-making and behavior patterns. We are all examples, and some of us are warnings. We all, at one time or another, impact other people. This is one of the reasons why I stress that it is so important to live consciously and be an example.

When I ask people about their belief systems and the habits and patterns that basically control their lives, I am often struck by how few of these beliefs and habits were ever chosen by that person on a conscious level. In other words, the rules that are guiding your life about how to BE in your own life very often picked up unconsciously.

It is incredible how common it is that people start this process, and when they begin to reassess their lives and their relationships with themselves and others in the success they are having or perhaps not having, they discover that much of what has been screwing up their lives, their achievements, their finances, their careers, their intimate relationships, and even their bodies (and I am not talking about the excuse many of us use about genetics. Being the reason, our bodies look the way they do) was influenced by their PARENTS. Not by their parents' problems necessarily, but by somehow trying to be liked, loved or appreciated by one parent. Many times, these decisions also have to do with trying to avoid pain that was inflicted by a parent or other significant role model, or simply standing up to a parent.

We can be 4050. Even 80 years old, and we are still living the strategies of a child.

And what's even worse, is it very often when we were a kid, we said, "I'll never be like that!" And here you are today, exactly like that! You don't want to admit it but if you held up a mirror and watched a film of your interactions you would say, "Oh my God, I never wanted to be like that parent." And yet you are. Or perhaps you have done the opposite. Perhaps you have thrown the pendulum the other way and you're not like that parent at all. Now, you are something worse. Or, let's just say you are something else. You are the opposite of the extreme you didn't like. And so now you are another extreme, that doesn't work either. Because no one teaches us this stuff, and so it becomes unconscious. We don't even see it. It's part of the invisible fabric of our thinking and our decision-making every single day.

This book will give you a unique opportunity to look deep inside yourself. It will allow you to look inside of your relationships, your decisions about money, and your decisions about your career, your relationship with God or your higher power, and even your body. It will allow you to understand how your own up bringing us may be influenced you and you probably know a lot of the ways it has influenced you, but maybe you'll spot some of the decisions you have made, maybe even one core decision that has affected your identity.

So, what the heck does identity mean anyway? It can be such a big and often loaded word. Well, I believe identity is the strongest force in the human personality. If you want to know what shapes you the most it's not your capability. It's your identity and the rules you have for who you think you are.

And you know what the challenge is? Most of us defined ourselves a long time ago. And when we step outside that definition, we get really uncomfortable, because the strongest force in the human personality is the need to remain consistent with how we define ourselves. Later, we will talk about the human needs referred to earlier. One of them is certainty. What this means is that if certainty is one of the deepest needs we have, then if you don't know who you are, you do not know how to act.

Very early in life, we begin to define who we are. We use labels such as loner, aggressive conservative, sexy, successful loser rich poor in charge. I work for others. I am ugly. I am smart. I am a procrastinator. I am clumsy. I am athletic. I am thin. I am big boned. What happens is these definitions become self-fulfilling prophecies, because nobody wants to be disappointed. Nobody wants to live in a place of uncertainty. So, there may be arranging your identity or in your definition of yourself, but it may not be absolute.

The metaphor that you so often hear what we talk about our comfort zone, is that our comfort zone is like a thermostat. We all have our comfort zone, and it is set by our subconscious mind. So, if your subconscious mind has set your thermostat in a particular area of your life, for example how much money you make, that let's say 45°, and if the temperature drops down to 40°, guess what happens? It doesn't meet your identity. In other words, things are not good enough, whether it be mentally and emotionally financially with your weight (which by the way is the primary reason people whose weight tend to gain it back because they lose it before reprogramming their subconscious mind to reset the thermostat) or whatever.

For example, if you drop down to 40° and your finances and 45° is your identity. This means that 45° is what you must have. Or, if you drop down to 70° in your intimacy and 80° is your identity, then this is what you must have. Whatever it is, when you drop below your comfort zone, you will be compelled to drive to make it better automatically. If your body gets out of control, there is a point at which you go, "that's enough!" You are willing to be a little off your identity but not that much. And suddenly you go on the diet suddenly make the change because you feel the pressure that comes with being inconsistent with your own definition of how you think you should be.

But what most of us fail to recognize is that this happens on the other side as well. Your subconscious mind since your mental thermostat at say 45° for your finances or 80° mentally for how close you want to be with your intimate partner, or 70° for how your body should look and feel,

This is not your *goal*. Your goal is something much larger. This is your subconscious comfort zone or your subconscious definition of yourself. For example, you might think of yourself as big boned, but if it suddenly isn't good enough and you really become overweight, then you change to fit your self-image or your definition of yourself in order to get back into that comfort zone. But also, if it gets better than you expected, perhaps, you lose a lot of weight and get really good shape, or perhaps you lead your company in sales for two quarters in a row when you normally come in third or fourth, or perhaps you jump from 70° in your intimacy, and now you have a relationship that is at 90 or even 100°. You have a really hot, passionate relationship with more passion than you ever have before, or you lose three dress sizes instead of one, or you double your income, whatever it is, your subconscious mind starts talking some sense into you. And your brain goes, "Hello, dude what the heck are you doing? You are 70 degree-er, what in heck are you doing way appear at 90? You can't keep that. That's not gonna last. Get back down to 70° before you get hurt or fail or screw it up. You're in over your head. You're not an entrepreneur. You work for other people."

Wherever your subconscious mind has set your comfort zone based on the way you define yourself, you're going to keep adjusting to stay in that comfort zone. So many times, in these types of programs, people challenge you to get out of your comfort zone, which you can't do consciously. You have to go into your subconscious and reset your comfort zone, just like you would the thermostat. And this will keep happening until you reprogram your subconscious mind with a new identity, and the new comfort zone. Before you set out to make any kind of lasting change, you must reset your subconscious comfort zone.

And what do we do when we exceed our comfort zone? Well, what happened is that the drive to make things better stops. And so you stop growing and gradually you drift back until you reach your comfort zone. Or worse, you start to sabotage. The mental air conditioners kick on and bring yourself right back down to where you think you deserve to be based on your subconscious identity.

For example, if the only kind of love you view as a child was abuse, the only kind of life. You knew was living paycheck to paycheck or in debt, or the only kind of lifestyle you ever experienced with sedentary, whatever it is, even though it might be painful. It is what you know. This becomes your comfort zone and therefore provides the certainty that you need. It becomes your self-definition and what you think you deserve. You begin to think -- not consciously, but unconsciously -- this IS love, this is just the body. You inherited, or that wealth is for other kinds of people, or you're not the right kind of person to make certain kinds of social contacts. Of course, this is not your conscious thinking that this is what is going on in your subconscious.

And therein lays the trouble, or perhaps a better way to say it, the shortcomings with many of the programs you may have tried in the past. They pump you up and felt good about it. They motivated you with affirmations and taught you use visualization. They've even taught you that the universal laws work for everyone. You may have even made some changes, but they did not last. Because when you're taught these things, you know the stuff in your head on a conscious level. But your identity and self-definition is the thermostat of subconscious mind, so before you can make any substantive or lasting change, first you must reprogram your subconscious mind and change who you are at the deepest level. (Green papers).

In other words, you must become the kind of person who has whatever it is that you want. Visualizing it, affirming it, and even living your life by a new set of standards is not going to work long term until this stuff goes from your conscious to your unconscious and finally into your heart. Not only do you have to DO it, and not only do you have to LIVE it, but you also have to BECOME it. And then you will manifest it.

And that is the difference between the stick figure you are drawing now or the paint by numbers life you have been taught to lead and the masterpiece you are now creating. So for the colors in our masterpiece is to really live consciously, to be an example, then we have to get conscious about what is shaping us and the thing that shapes you most identity.

Someone who is outrageous will behave, say things differently and move differently than someone who believes they are extremely conservative. They will use a different voice, a different way of moving and a different language. Here is my question for you:

When did you come up with this definition?

When did you decide that is who you are?

When was the last time you updated it?

Maybe it's time to take another look at who you are today. And maybe you don't have to actually give up your identity. Maybe the identity created for yourself is magnificent, but maybe it's time to expand it. Maybe it's time to add to it. Maybe it's time to open up to a new level of freedom and options.

And when you do that there will be a processional effect in all areas of your life, because we are all connected in a cybernetic loop. If I want to change you, I can try to control you, but that will not change anything. Or I can try to change the system, but that will not last or will be futile. Or I can change me into an ID that everything changes.

For example, if I change the way I treat you the way I respond to you my voice my body my feelings and my emotions by respect for you. It will affect the way you feel and the way you respond back. And the same is true with the universe and higher intelligence. Once you change yourself, reprogram your subconscious, become the person you need to become that the things that you want in your life, then you will begin to receive a different response from the universe in a different result in your life. Then begin to experience your life as a masterpiece.

You will learn that what we value controls what we are willing to do or not do -- in our businesses, and our relationships, with our bodies and with her children. Some people get locked in place into a mindset. I call it being committed to your commitment. For example, have you ever been in an argument, and you were so angry that as the argument progressed, you forgot what you were angry about, and it just became about winning? We've all been there and what happens is we get committed to being angry and said that resolving the argument. Or we get committed to being right, instead of uncovering the truth. When this happens, get so wrapped up in our commitment that we can no longer see the forest through the trees. We lose touch with what we really want, because we get stuck in a mindset, and we get committed to our commitments.

(Judy- discovers a decision she made as a child and uses the discovery to transform her life and her children and grandchildren's lives).

Today, you are beginning a process that can truly change the quality of your life forever and can take that paint by numbers life you might be living now and create the masterpiece called your life. So just for a moment now, what I want you to do is imagine that your life is a painting. And imagine that you have died and are looking down at that painting. What did you leave behind? Is your life, a masterpiece that is cherished and hangs prominently as an example for others of what is possible, or is it a paint-by-numbers life that is packed away in someone's basement?

As you begin this process, I asked for only two things from you:

1. Your heartfelt desire to make real changes.

2. The commitment to follow through and do this, as simple or as located as it might seem in the moment.

If you can do just those two things, then the things that you used to call dreams will become part of your daily reality.

Why is it that you can have a person who seems to have superior abilities, talents, skills, and education, the same time, they don't produce the quality of life they want or that you might expect from them? And why is it, on the other hand, you can have someone who seemingly has every disadvantage -- no family support, the wrong social status, no emotional support, no education, and the wrong background -- and yet they go out and produce results, way beyond what anyone could have expected or even imagined?

The difference in our quality of life is not about our capability, background or education. Human beings, *that means you*, are *all capable* of achieving incredible results, and yet sadly only a few seem to get it.

What people WILL do is very different from what people CAN do.

I want to challenge you right now to start using your WILL muscle, instead of your TRY muscle, which is probably overdeveloped anyhow. I challenge you to start exercising your inborn human power, which is your birthright as a member of the human race, your ability to act based on the choice and free will that every human has in equal measure. Frankly, this means that if it has been achieved, then there is no reason on earth why you cannot achieve it. And beyond that, if it can be imagined, then there is also very little reason why you cannot achieve it. As a matter of fact, your unconscious mind will rarely imagine something that you are capable of. That is the difference between desires and fantasies. It's true. There are no excuses anymore. If you are reading this and you are a human being that you have the ability to take action and to produce results.

The disability that I'm talking about is not something I can give you. Why? Because you already have it. You were born, great. Now, I challenge you to go out and take back what is rightfully yours.

Hopefully, something is now a weekend within you in two ways. One, by igniting your desire and two by showing you some simple systematic strategies on how you can get greater results out of yourself on a daily basis.

When most of us think of success or failure, we tend to think of these monumental things. Failure is not an overnight thing, and neither is success.

Just what is success? Well, some people describe it in terms of achievements like our resume. But it is different for everyone. So some people describe it as a feeling. It's your difficult for you to make it a goal to achieve a feeling for something that is difficult to define. Many programs attempt to do that, and they use motivation to give you that temporary feeling of success. But it doesn't last.

The truth is that success is actually wrapped up in failure. What I mean by that is that success is simply a string of failures all going in the same purposeful direction. That's right. If you want to find success you have to look inside a failure. In other words, if you want to be more successful than the next person, then you simply have to be willing to experience more failure, but not just any failures. You must be willing to take specific actions, based on specific decisions, fail most of the time, keep going, perhaps with a new strategy, experience and more failures, and eventually you will succeed. If this sounds painful, then I want you to think for a moment about what true failure actually is.

True failure is lifelong failure. It is the failure of inactivity. It's not actually failing at what you DO -- those things will lead to success. But when you fail to DO, you fail to succeed. In failing to do is a recipe for ultimate failure in life. When you fail to make the calls, when you fail to follow through, when you fail to say I love you, when you fail to give your all, that is what creates the ultimate failure in life. Ultimate failure creates the greatest pain, the feelings we want to avoid at all costs. Now *that* is painful.

Success happens one step at a time. Success happens one failure at a time. It is successfully making the calls and doing it no matter how long it takes for the outcome in the moment. It is successfully getting up and following through. It is successfully making sure that you make that unique contact. It is successfully breaking through the limits that used to stop you.

Success is a combination of all those little things -- those little successes that often come disguised as failures -- over each day and over your lifetime that eventually create a life that you will have total pride and great joy in knowing that you created your life and made it into a masterpiece of your very own -- a life that is an example to others as how it is done.

The purpose of Life Masterpiece is to show you how to tap the power you were born with and how to tap into it every single day. And to make it an effortless process so that it becomes a lifestyle.

Before I go any further, I want to thank you for your friendship. Even though I have never met you, personally, I feel as if you and I are kindred spirits. The reason why say that is it you picked up this book. You made an investment. You're now reading it. This means you are one of the few who will do what others will not. This puts you light years ahead of 99% of the people. You and I encounter every day. Those people are living a paint-by-numbers life. They want to change, but they just do not get it, because they haven't got the first clue what they want and worse, they are not willing to do anything to change it.

I know you're special because you are researching and exploring and because you are reading this. It says something to me about you. It tells me that you are willing to do what it takes to succeed. It tells me that you are not satisfied with your life, and you will not be satisfied until you have successfully created your own masterpiece. So, I really want to give you the tools that can make a difference.

I have dedicated my life to understanding what makes people do what they do. What drives you? What is it that makes the difference in performance from one human being to the next? If we are all born with the same stuff, what causes some to tap into it and others to settle for a mediocre, paint-by-numbers existence?

Power comes from concentrating your focus and taking daily action to improve something. Even a 1% improvement today can result in unbelievable change, because 1% per day will not give you a 365% difference in being the year, because it builds and compounds to create a difference, way beyond anything you can probably imagine right now.

I will show you how to make it happen quickly, not 10 or 20 years from now, but today. Anything you commit to and focus on everyday must improve.

The challenge is that most of us do not know WHO we are, and therefore do not know how to control our mental focus. In fact, most of us focus on what is not working and spent most of her energy focusing on what we DON'T want by asking questions like, "how come this always happens to me?" If you focus on that enough, then that is what you will continue to experience. (Universal laws don't work unless you reprogram).

I am going to show you how to refocus your mental energy and reprogram your subconscious, so that you can ask better questions and therefore get a better result. Whatever you focus on, you manifest, which is why the Law of attraction won't work until you know what you want at the deepest level of your mind.

The key is to get you to live by those factors. Most people focus on the small stuff. I know you are to believe this, or you would not have picked up this book. Most people are so focused on what they have to DO. In other words, they focus on their to-do list, how to make a living instead of how to create their life. You could so easily get caught up in the day-to-day experiences that you tend to make a monument of the port in your mind, when actually in the long term these things that seem monumentally important now are actually quite trivial.

To create your masterpiece, you have to learn how to take care of the big things -- each color in your crayon box -- mentally, emotionally, physically, financially, and spiritually. Here are two things that usually lead to ultimate success -- either inspiration or desperation. Desperation can be a good thing because until you get really dissatisfied. You won't do anything to take your life to another level. Dissatisfaction is awesome! If you are completely satisfied, you will get comfortable. They may life begins to deteriorate.

My guess is that you invested in this book because on some level you are dissatisfied.

("If you make enough money, at least you can handle your problems in style" R)

(lots of money, beyond comfort zone)

"It's a funny thing, the more I practice the luckier I get" AP

Subconsciously, most of us have an idea of what we think we deserve. This is our comfort zone, which the subconscious mind determines when it sets our internal thermostat. Your subconscious mind has set your internal thermostat, and so when you begin to achieve, perhaps make a lot of money, you begin to sabotage your success dropping down to where you subconsciously think you deserve to be.

The past does not equal the future. Even if you are jaded and cynical, you've tried everything, this moment is a great new opportunity if you've tried other programs in the past that nothing has really changed your lifelong term. I believe that all it has done is it has prepared you for this program. And at some level if you did not believe that, then you would not be reading this right now.

Life Masterpiece is very different from other programs you may have tried. You will not find affirmations and visualizations and motivations in this book. What you will find is the answer to what is keeping you back, and how to reprogram your subconscious mind and how to use it to create.

Your brain is the most powerful computer on the planet. When you learn to use it properly, you can create any result you want. And they can give you the answer to almost any problem you have. The problem is that this computer, we call our brain is not user-friendly, and does not come with an owner's manual. Life Masterpiece will show you how to operate your supercomputer with precision. Lasting change is not created in your life by learning more. Lasting change is created by using your own power to take action.

We're going to recondition the way your mind works by reprogramming your subconscious. This will change the way you feel and the way you behave for the rest of your life. Just as there have been extraordinary technological, scientific and medical breakthroughs in the past two decades there has also been a breakthrough in the science of quantum physics. While we are not going to learn specifically about quantum physics in this book, we are going to take and use part of that technology. Because the latest cutting-edge tools for creating lasting change comes from breakthroughs in quantum physics that have to do with human technology and how to get new results in record time.

There are four steps to success:

1. Know what you want. It is important for you to know what you want, and for you to know how you want things to turn out. In other words, you must know your outcome before you begin. The first step is to decide what you want out of whatever situation you are currently in. The clearer you aren't what you want, the more you will empower your brain to give you the answers.

2. You must use it. In other words, you must get yourself to take action toward your outcome. This means that you must put energy in the right direction, even when you do not know exactly what to do. Many people do not know what to do first. I will teach you exactly what to do. Some

people want to know what happens if they try, and it doesn't work. I can tell you right now, and you will learn why in this book, why nothing you try will ever work. So how do you take action? Decide to. It's not about what you can do. It's about what you will do.

3. Notice your results. It's not enough to take action. You must also pay attention to the results you are getting from your actions. Do your actions always work? No. Remember, success is just a series of failures, but failures with the purpose, failures directed at a specific result. You know what you want; you took action, now notice the result. (JS-obstacles and timing).

4. Be flexible and willing to change your approach. You must be willing to make changes and adjustments based on the results of your actions, because flexibility is the key to the system. In other words, if you notice that what you are doing is not working. And you're not getting closer to your goal or even getting further away, instead of feeling like a failure in giving up. Sometimes you simply need to change your approach.

There is a way to speed this up. Instead of just knowing what you want, taking random actions, I will show you a way to increase the pace and the certainty of your success.

("Knowledge is not power. Knowledge is potential power." R)

You may be thinking, "Jim, if this is a simple, how come everyone isn't doing it?" The answer is because the majority of people tend to get caught up in the day-to-day trivialities such as paying their bills. Now, paying your bills might seem monumentally important to you, but honestly, can you think of anyone who has ever reported that they were successful in life because they mastered the art of bill paying? I am not saying that you shouldn't pay your bills, what I'm saying is that you should know I yourself to get caught up in something trivial and make it something big, so that you can use it as an excuse for not doing the really important things in life. At the end of your life, no one is going to remember whether or not you paid all of your bills and what a wonderful job you did of it. In other words, people get caught up in making a living instead of creating a life. They come to the end of their life dissatisfied because they realize they only live 10% of it, not because they were not capable or intelligent, and not for a lack of knowledge, but simply because they never had a clear idea about what they wanted.

Some people think that what they really want is a program that deals with only one area of your life like that business program. If that is what you are thinking, let me tell you right now that Life Masterpiece is one of the most powerful business programs because it deals with the source of all your business -- YOU. When you are better will be a better speaker, salesperson negotiator. Your creativity will flow freely. Mobile to manage and influence people far more effectively than you can now. The first step to changing your career and your business is to change yourself.

***

www.lutesinternational.com

info@lutesinternational.com

https://www.facebook.com/jimlutes

https://mindmotionacademy.com

Dr. Elizabeth Ssemanda

Are you ready to bring about positive change in the world? Dr. Elizabeth Ssemanda is certainly prepared to do it! She's a medical intuitive, psychiatrist, and life coach with an impressive academic background that includes degrees from Brown University (undergraduate, masters & medical doctorate), Johns Hopkins Bloomberg School of Public Health (PhD in Clinical Trials Epidemiology), and psychiatry residency at the University of Michigan–Ann Arbor.

Dr. Ssemanda is dedicated to offering a holistic approach to healing, with an emphasis on helping healers, caregivers, and empaths. She is especially interested in improving the experiences of expectant and existing parents and brings a great amount of expertise to the table as a psychiatrist, having worked in various environments – most notably, emergency services during the COVID-19 crisis. Dr. Ssemanda is devoted to supporting individuals through their unique struggles, offering her knowledge and guidance.

Drawing upon her understanding of the battles that many face, Dr. Ssemanda has established two practices to promote healing and wholeness: New U Psychiatry, which provides mental health and wellness services, and Soulinyou, offering intuitive readings, coaching, and healing.

Dr. Ssemanda is also the proud host of Stepping into Soul Power—a podcast meant to revolutionize how people approach mental wellbeing. Her invaluable knowledge and advice assist her audience to eliminate blocks, improve relationships, and obtain harmony of mind, body, and soul.

The 7 Mental Health Secrets to Manifesting Your Desires Faster

By Dr. Elizabeth Ssemanda

Introduction

Are you looking to make a lasting impact in the world? Do you have ambitions and goals that seem out of reach? You will be happy to know there are tangible steps you can take to bring your dreams and aspirations closer. Manifestation of your true desires is an attractive yet challenging feat; many people struggle for years on how to consistently achieve their desired results. They do not understand the importance of mental health in manifesting their goals. The exciting news is that there are things you (yes, you) can do to get the results you want faster. Good mental wellness can help you unlock opportunities and stay motivated while achieving your accelerated desired outcomes. Poor mental health can prevent any progress and even sabotage efforts toward goal achievement. It is well known that a heighted sense of fear and negativity have become pervasive in our world. Even the World Health Organization acknowledges a significant rise in global anxiety levels.[1] As an experienced psychiatrist, medical intuitive, and life coach, I understand how vital mental wellness is for individuals looking to achieve personal goals in a timely manner. Change is possible. I hope that, by raising awareness and offering practical strategies for promoting mental wellbeing, we can create a world where all may truly experience greater wellbeing and manifest their dreams faster. Manifesting one's dreams and living authentically is not only beneficial for an individual, but for everyone. We are interconnected. The lives of one touch the lives of many. Aware of this, I am keen on helping you make your dreams come true by providing you with seven mental health secrets to aid in achieving the dreams you desire faster. My framework comes from psychological, spiritual, and personal development principles, all used with the goal of accelerating your manifestation. Read on to find out more about my secrets that can help you manifest your dreams quicker!

Mental Health Secret #1: Believe That You Are the Determining Factor in Your Manifestation

Breaking news: The course of your life is truly in your hands! You must see yourself as the creator of your reality. Your thoughts are incredibly powerful. Whether it be matters of mental health or pursuing personal ambitions, you can shape these aspects of your life however you choose by reframing how you think. When unfortunate incidents occur, think not of them as obstacles but possibilities for growth—opportunities to become ever stronger and more determined. Assume responsibility for yourself and take charge of your thoughts. You can choose what thoughts to focus on; what thoughts to give your energy to. If you give your attention to something, it will gain energy, and the more energy it gets, the more it will grow. It is only through such a mindset that big dreams can come to fruition. To achieve your objectives and make a positive impact, it is essential to manage your thoughts. Reframing, or writing your story as if you are the leading protagonist of your life's movie, is an effective technique for taking ownership of what happens in your world. When you consider yourself the star performer in this play, you no longer see external forces acting upon you—you are the one who determines and creates each plot point that occurs. Have self-efficacy, believe that you can do it. Take charge of our thoughts, write the story of your life in an empowering way. You possess incredible power within, believe it. Embedded deep within is a vast capacity for crafting your aspirations. Imbue yourself with confidence–trust that through determination and you can make tremendous changes!

Mental Health Secret #2: Pay Attention to the Patterns in Your Life

When you go on a road trip with a destination in mind, most of us like to know of any roadblocks or traffic jams so we can make detours to reach our destination quickly. The patterns in your life will provide you with insight into any blocks to manifesting. You must understand them if you are going to manifest your dreams faster. It is a fact that we are always manifesting. Whether we are aware of it, consciously or subconsciously. In the psychological community, it's been postulated that we are only conscious of a meager portion of our thoughts and behaviors; the remainder is out of our awareness or not yet conscious.[2] It's important to look for patterns in your life that appear time and time again. These may be behaviors, emotional experiences, and thoughts. Your patterns can serve as blueprints from which you can identify what you are manifesting without realizing. So, take a few minutes to examine the various situations you find yourself in frequently. Do you keep ending up in similar relationships? Do certain arguments recur with different people? Do any negative feelings appear repeatedly? Digging within will help you comprehend recurring themes, so you gain knowledge and use that data as power to bring about the circumstances you truly want to manifest.

It is important to take a step back and evaluate the things we are doing that could hold us back from achieving our goals. Taking the time to assess one's behaviors and patterns can be difficult, as obligations and requests from others that demand our attention constantly bombard us. It is easy to become distracted and focus on the external world, but it is crucial for personal growth to pay attention to what is happening within us. Tune into the subtle messages your life is telling you, and think about those patterns, both conscious and unconscious, that may stand in your way of progress. If you have trouble identifying patterns, it is perfectly fine to ask for help. Sometimes, others can pinpoint things about us we cannot. Exploration and knowledge of one's patterns can open a realm to creative solutions. By showing kindness to yourself and taking the time to reflect on your patterns, you take the first step toward conscious solutions. Patterns are not a sign of failure; rather, they provide a chance for growth and understanding. Meaningful change starts with awareness. Self-awareness of our patterns gives us the power to respond thoughtfully instead of reacting emotionally.

Mental Health Secret #3: Stop Running from Your Emotions

Our emotional state affects our ability to manifest, so it is time to think strategically about managing your emotions. Rather than seeing them as something we should fear, suppress, or ignore, we must understand emotions are simply information. Your emotions offer insights into how closely your current life mirrors your heart's deepest desires. This is especially important for manifesting what you want in life. Certain negative emotional states, such as guilt, shame, depression, or fear, make it much harder for you to manifest what you desire. The law of attraction suggests that like begets like. The positive emotions that one emits will draw more of the same towards them. So, if you want to attract more joy and love into your life, then it is essential to foster a high-vibrational state of love and bliss. Nowadays, the natural response is often either to repress these negative feelings or to run from them. We may use drugs, technology, work, and food to distract ourselves from feelings. Instead, we need to recognize the value of our emotions and learn how best to work with them. Understand and recognize your emotions. Ask yourself what you're feeling and what you need. Psychiatric experts call this the "opposite action": if sadness tempts us to isolate, reach out for comfort and loving support instead. If anger arises from a sense of injustice, hear it, but seek active listening to confirm your feelings rather than reacting with additional aggression. Acknowledging your emotions and recognizing the entire range of what it means to be human is essential for manifesting your goals. If you are determined to create the life you really want, then you must face and accept your feelings. You should start by being mindful; paying attention in a non-judgmental way on purpose can help in understanding them. Learning how to recognize each feeling will give you information about what you need. You can use that knowledge to move to a higher vibration emotion. Naming these emotions as you experience them is key.

Ultimately, consciousness and recognition of one's emotions lets us know ourselves better so we can make changes for true happiness. Set an intention to accept and release lower vibration emotions, then transition to emotions with higher vibration states, such as gratitude, love, or joy. Gratitude, joy, and love are often the emotions we want to experience when we manifest a dream. Getting into these higher vibration states attracts these dreams to us. Unconditional acceptance is an embodiment of love, while joy signifies happiness, pleasure, contentment, and greater confidence in the moment. These powerful emotions assist in consciously manifesting work. There is an incredibly helpful technique to consider when an unfortunate event occurs. It is the five-minute rule. Basically, when you have something unfortunate happen, allow yourself to feel that and let the emotion go through you. Next, choose to reframe the experience positively and finally focus on something you are genuinely grateful for. This will help raise your vibration and assist in bringing conditions that match the much sought after higher vibration experiences to you.

Mental Health Secret #4: Let Your Spirit Guide You

When in sync with our spirit, we can manifest goals more quickly. One telltale sign that you are in sync is that life becomes easier and more effortless. You move into a state of flow. If you feel you are facing resistance or difficulty in achieving your goals, this could indicate that you are not operating in line with what your soul desires. The universe will provide feedback. A song you hear or a story you read later in the day may be relevant to you—it is important to listen and adjust accordingly. Taking time out to pause and reflect can provide insight into our soul's purpose. Meditating, the act of training your awareness and attention, is one way to do this, as it allows us to access the deeper wisdom and knowledge within ourselves. If we sit with ourselves in stillness and ask ourselves what our mission in this lifetime is, our intuition often reveals insights useful for achieving clarity on why we are here. It is important to trust what emerges from within, as we are ultimately the expert on our lives. After all, you spend every moment with yourself! When meditating, one important technique people have found helpful is to tune into the heart. The heart is truly a compass. It is the guide to what your spirit wants. And taking time and the space to tune into the heart, meditate, and ask what it wants is an exceptional way to navigate life. When you tune into the heart, you are listening to what your spirit wants. And achieving alignment with your soul not only offers clarity of your purpose but makes you more likely to experience life in a flow state. For many, being in flow is associated with a higher vibration emotional state, so manifestation occurs faster.

Mental Health Secret #5: Create a Sacred Space That Fosters Joy

Our environment influences our ability to manifest what we desire. It is important to be aware of the connection we have with our surroundings. Colors, shapes, and other items nearby can impact us without our noticing. With manifesting goals and dreams, this is especially true. Ask yourself how your current environment makes you feel. Do you feel inspired? Joyful? On the lower end of the spectrum; angry, guilty, or sad? If it is the latter, consider changes that could help create a more inspiring atmosphere. Do a survey of your space and note sensations, feelings, and thoughts as you go through each item. Pay attention. Sometimes these are small but impactful shifts! Take this "intuitive information" as a cue to change your space. I am an advocate of having a place, just for you, where you can feel secure and be your true self. Bring products that emphasize joy, thankfulness, serenity, and love into your sacred space. Struggling for inspiration? Tap into the artist inside you. Draw pictures or get creative with natural materials. The environment we are in affects us deeply. It's not just physical aspects but non-physical elements such as lighting, smells, and sounds influence our well-being, too. Use both physical and nonphysical items to create an atmosphere of contentment. You can change the surrounding vibes! Being in a peaceful area heightens the power of manifestation.

Mental Health Secret #6: Embrace Focus as Your Superpower

Conscious manifestation requires focus. To achieve dreams, it is important to have a clear vision of what we want. Having multiple goals can be beneficial, but in manifesting these goals, the power is in concentrated focus. The more goals you add to manifestation, the longer it takes. You are essentially giving the universe a mixed message. Be clear and show the universe you are certain of what you want to manifest in your life. Attend to one thing and keep your thoughts centered on that goal. Do not give up if results do not appear quickly. Instead, use meditation and visualization techniques to stay focused. Regularly see, feel, and taste what it would be like to manifest that goal. See how it would benefit you and others. Remind yourself of the power of your thoughts to create your reality; the more you visualize success with a particular manifestation, the more likely it is for you to achieve it.

For many people, learning how to focus can be a long-term process. As with running a marathon, it takes time and effort to develop the skills. Regular meditation is one way of do that; no matter where you are or what you are doing, there are opportunities for meditation. For centuries, meditation has been utilized to hone the recognition of the here and now. Fundamentally, it is a practice where one directs their attention to reflect on a single object, sound, picture, or experience. It is possible to meditate while on a walk, dining, or even in a stationary position. Creativity is the only limit for the type of mediation goals you can aim for. Allocating even five minutes daily can be helpful in making continuous progress to building your focus.

Mental Health Secret #7: Cultivate Trust in the Universe

To manifest faster, we must have faith in the universe. Change from a mindset of lack to that of abundance. Many of us have grown up in environments where we act like crabs in a barrel, believing there is only a limited supply of abundance available. Our thoughts create our reality. If we believe that the universe is abundant, it will be. Manifesting faster requires faith that the universe will provide. When we focus on what we lack, the law of attraction deems that is what we want and sends us more circumstances where we lack. When we trust in the universe's power, instead of succumbing to fear and doubt, we create a stronger, more powerful, divine bond. One way to build trust so you can manifest faster is to start small with your manifestation goals. In the beginning, start off by manifesting something trivial, something you are ambivalent about, that you are not heavily invested in emotionally. When you ask the universe for it, focus on being in a positive emotional state. Trust that the universe will provide, and it will. As your smaller manifestations come to fruition, work your way up to bigger goals of manifestation. Nothing builds trust like experience. And the more you see you can manifest consciously, the stronger your faith and trust in the universe becomes.

Take Home Points

To manifest effectively, it is essential to remember the importance of our mental wellness. Our mindset and mental health affect our ability to manifest what we want and achieve success. Pay attention to the patterns in your life; they can help you identify your personal blocks and opportunities for growth and manifestation. Do not be afraid of facing your emotions head on! Emotions contain invaluable data that can help you move closer toward your goals if you allow yourself to feel them without judgement or fear and use them as data to inform what your next steps should be. Ultimately, if you are trying to bring a goal into your life through conscious manifestation, it is important to nurture high-vibration emotional states. If you are not feeling in a high-vibrational state, take note and assess what may be the cause. You may need to pause and listen more closely to your spirit. A conflict between your spirit and your manifestation goals can impede successful manifestation. Focusing on one goal in alignment with your spirit is critical. To foster an optimal environment for manifesting, we recommend embracing feelings of joy, love, and gratitude. Not only will these help you achieve success faster, but also enjoy every step of your journey to achieving your dreams.

***

To contact Dr. Ssemanda

Book a healing session at: https://soulinyou.com

Learn more at: https://www.newupsychiatry.com

LinkedIn: https://www.linkedin.com/in/elizabeth-ssemanda-04aa9074/

Facebook:
1) https://www.facebook.com/inspiresoulinyou
2) https://www.facebook.com/newupsychiatry

Instagram:
1) https://www.instagram.com/inspiresoulinyou/
2) https://www.instagram.com/newupsychiatry/

YouTube: http://www.youtube.com/inspiresoulinyou

Podcast: Stepping into Soul Power is available on iTunes, Spotify, Anchor, Amazon, and Google Podcasts

References:

1. World Health Organization. (2022, March 2). *COVID-19 pandemic triggers 25% increase in prevalence of anxiety and depression worldwide*. World Health Organization. https://www.who.int/news/item/02-03-2022-covid-19-pandemic-triggers-25-increase-in-prevalence-of-anxiety-and-depression-worldwide

2. Harley, T. A. (2021). *The science of consciousness: waking, sleeping and dreaming.* Cambridge University Press.

Rachel Best

Rachel is a keynote motivational speaker, founder of How to Make Your Mark in the World, and author, podcaster, and empowerment mindset coach.

She is the owner of a personal development company as a Certified Neuro-linguistic Empowerment Mindset coach. She is also certified in Timeline Therapy. She helps her clients overcome mindset blocks and limiting beliefs to identify what is holding them back from walking in their true purpose and potential, to let go of what is holding them back, to reprogram their minds, and to make big moves in their life.

Her passion is to awaken individuals in how to make their mark in the world, find their signature, and use their gifts, talents, and life experiences.

Rachel is Married with five kids ranging from 7-25 and has two grandsons.

Her favorite things to do are to be with family and to travel the country. In September 2021, her husband Josh, youngest son Maverick, and Rachel decided to sell their home to live full-time in their RV.

Being by the ocean, palm trees, and sun fills her soul.

From Dreamer to Achiever
Making a Mark in the World

By Rachel Best

"Your message has the power to change lives, and it is up to you to take it to the world, To Make Your Mark in the World. You get to decide how this will happen." – Rachel Best

When I was a young girl in my hometown of Delphos, Ohio, a community of fewer than 7000 people, I had a big dream and vision for life—growing up in a quiet town where not much happened, surrounded by fields and forests. For as long as I can remember, I was curious about the world beyond this small town. My imagination took me to places I had never been, and I dreamed of seeing the bright lights of big cities and experiencing diverse cultures. I daydreamed about traveling to different locations while taking in all the sights and sounds.

As a little girl in my bedroom playing with Barbie dolls' hair, I was filled with a dream that I would do hair and makeup. I wanted to do celebrities' hair in Hollywood. But life took an unexpected turn when I became pregnant and then a mother as a sophomore in high school at 17 to my first-born son Devin. As you can only imagine, many looked down upon my situation, but by God's grace, I not only graduated high school with an 18-month child on my hip, but I also earned my cosmetology license. Despite the challenges, I refused to give up on my dreams.

My parents always said I was rebellious and pushed against the grain. They called it "rebellious." I saw it as "determination." All I knew was that I wanted to accomplish great things in life. My hope was to make what I saw in my mind and felt in my heart. I became a great multitasker. All the while, I worked nearly full-time for a fast-food restaurant while staying in school and raising a baby. Devin, his father, and I lived at my parents' house throughout my junior year of high school. By my mid-senior year, we were able to get a small apartment near my parents.

After high school, I married my high school boyfriend, Devin's father. By the age of 22, I had three children, all under the age of five. We were a struggling young family trying to pay all the bills, diapers, formula, and handle babysitting. Can you imagine the stress that added to life? Knowing we needed more space, we moved to a village named Spencerville in Ohio. We went from a tiny town to an even smaller one with only one stoplight. I knew I had to do what it took to survive, so I started working as a makeup artist and hair stylist at a hair salon. During this time, we were so poor that we had no other alternative but to live on government assistance.

During my 7th year of marriage, my life took a turn when I came home from work to an empty house. My husband left and never returned. There was no goodbye. I was faced with the reality that I would raise our three children alone. This was the darkest time in my life. I found myself abandoned, depressed, and afraid of the unknown future I was forced to walk through. I had never planned it this way. I just knew his decision changed my and my three children's lives forever.

Soon after, I found myself making decisions I would regret. Once again, I found myself making a decision that would drastically alter my story, which would ultimately become my life's purpose. This pivotal moment shaped my journey and inspired me to share my story through my book "How to Make Your Mark in the World...Finding Your Signature."

On March 18, 2009, I had an encounter with Jesus, the one who would transform my life. From that day on, I have meditated on the Bible to teach and guide me. This is how my transformation has come to pass. My hope is to carry this decision with me for the rest of my life. I started saying "yes" to Jesus, one "yes" at a time. Through this, I have listened to His calling on my life and the obedience that has led me to go where He guides me and do what he asks. I find comfort in the bible verse:

1 Thessalonians 5:16-18 says, "Rejoice always, pray without ceasing, give thanks in all circumstances; for this is the will of God in Christ Jesus for you."

Being a single mother was demanding. There were many obstacles I would need to overcome as it was a daily challenge. I understand that the road was a long, winding one that ultimately tested my strength, courage, and resilience. During those years, I lacked self-esteem, confidence and often found myself alone and overwhelmed trying to be both mom and dad to my children. At times I would want to give up, but the hope in reading the Word of God would give me the strength to push forward. I had faith that if I stayed true to God's calling, He would honor His promises. The blessing would come five years later, and I would meet my forever love. We became a blended family.

During the Spring of 2015, I found a health and wellness company that introduced me to Mindset and Personal Development. Besides my faith and the Bible, I had never been inspired and challenged to grow. I was never much of a reader in my younger years, as that was a challenge for me. In fact, the last books I read were those I had to read during my high school years. I knew this would not be easy; nevertheless, I accepted the challenge. I started digging into personal development books. Luckily this time, we had new technology in the world that allowed me to dive into audiobooks, YouTube, and podcasts. I discovered a new part of my life that I began to fall in love with, which helped me learn and grow.

Four years later, I attended a leadership summit that would change my life forever. While there, I heard God speaking to me. He told me that I needed to quit my hairstylist job and that I needed to pursue coaching full-time. I found myself at a crossroads. I loved my job as a hairstylist but knew God was calling me to do something bigger and greater. I remember several years before, when I got saved, I knew I would be sharing my testimony on a public stage someday. I was given a vision that I would become a public speaker who would inspire others to overcome obstacles, accomplish their dreams, and find their purpose.

I've always had big dreams. I refused to let what others told me "you can't" stop me from becoming the person I was created to be. The words "you can't" fueled me to prove them wrong. I would not let the narrative of "what not to be like" become a reality, but rather the story of redemption and who God created me to become. I knew I had to pursue my dreams, so I quit my full-time salon job of 20 years and decided to go all-in with the personal development, health, and wellness company. This was the vehicle that provided me the financial freedom to be at home with my family, along with the time that has allowed me to grow and learn in my faith and personal development.

As I dove deeper into pursuing personal development, I wanted to find the solutions and reasons why people get stuck. I became proficient in the understanding of our conscious and unconscious minds; in this, I found the pathway to get unstuck in all areas of one's life. I found an incredible program that would ultimately serve as the key to what I had been searching for.

As I began learning more about the factors that keep us from achieving our goals and how we can overcome limiting beliefs and traumas, I realized that my true calling was to help others do the same. Shortly before starting my certification classes, I envisioned a bicycle pedaling while shifting gears and then coming to an abrupt stop. Suddenly, the bike started to clunk and gain momentum once again. I heard God telling me that we were shifting gears. At that time, I had no idea what this meant, but over the next year and a half, it became abundantly clear that my next chapter in life was to launch my own Personal Development coaching business, become a paid speaker and author of many books. I would get to travel the world and pursue the dreams that had been stirring up inside of me for some time.

In 2021, I began speaking on stages, and it became clearer to me that my vision to become a keynote motivational speaker was becoming my reality. I can remember there was a very brief moment when I felt like I had missed the mark. After making endless phone calls to secure speaking engagements, I faced rejection after rejection and began to doubt myself. Once again, I turned to God, praying and seeking guidance about my next steps. One day I was working out while listening to Les Brown for inspiration. At that moment, I felt like he was speaking directly to me. In his words, I felt an overwhelming peace that confirmed speaking was my calling. I knew with certainty that I was on the right path. Looking back, I feel as if my faith was testing my commitment to push forward or give up.

The next day, to my surprise, a Facebook friend whom I had never met before reached out to me to connect on the phone. I received an invitation to be a part of his speaker comp. And I said yes. Leaving this competition, I left inspired. Weeks later, I was part of a mastermind that moved me to fully commit to focusing on making my mark with my story. Everything started to fall into place when my goal was to become a successful speaker.

My heart's desire is to share my story with many so that they, too, believe whatever they decide to commit to can come to fruition. It is not easy, as I have spent countless hours understanding and developing my message so that you would understand how you can have the same opportunity I have been given. My goal is to continue speaking on local to global platforms and virtual conferences, along with challenging myself to participate in speaker competitions and academies. My hope is to inspire individuals to overcome their setbacks in life while giving them hope and inspiration.

Many people carry their purpose, as I would say, in a backpack rather than in their heart. I have created a course to teach people how to "Make their Mark in the World." They will find their purpose using their gifts, talents, and life experiences. This course is designed to help individuals identify their passions and develop a plan to achieve their goals. In there, you will find tools for public speaking, crafting your message, and sharing it. You will learn all of the tools needed to succeed. In addition to the course, there will be speaking events and platforms worldwide by which all speakers will come together to share their passion for making a difference in the world as thought leaders. I aim to awaken the voice within, even those who did not know they had a story to share.

My ultimate vision is to have a non-profit that will host small intimate events that will awaken people to see their dreams as reality. My dream is to buy a house on the beach so I can invite others to experience growth and empowerment.

Did you know that our life, when transformed, can be much like the process of refining gold? Just as gold needs to be melted down and purified to become valuable, we, too, may need to go through a transformation process to reach our full potential. This process can involve breaking down old habits, beliefs, and behaviors that no longer serve us and replacing them with new ones that align with our values and aspirations.

Just as gold is heated to high temperatures to separate it from impurities, we may need to face intense challenges or difficult situations to shed our own negative qualities and become the best versions of ourselves. This process can be painful and uncomfortable, but it is necessary for personal growth and transformation. As gold is refined and transformed into something beautiful, we can emerge from our refining process as a more authentic, resilient, and fulfilled version of ourselves. This transformation can lead to greater joy, meaning, and purpose in our lives as we align with our true selves and live in harmony with our values.

A simple exercise to find your number one goal:

Write down five things you are passionate about. Now cross out two, now cross out two more. The remaining is your number one dream, goal, or desire. This is the motivating factor that will take you where you want to go. As you focus on just that one goal, the other goals will naturally fall into place.

1_____

2_____

3_____

4_____

5_____

5 Keys To Elevate Your Success:

1. Forgive and let go: Forgive yourself and others who have hurt you in the past. Holding grudges and resentments can hold you back from success.
2. Follow your path: Obey and follow the direction that God takes you. Trust that your path will lead you to your purpose.

3. Believe in yourself: Have faith and belief in yourself, and trust that what you hope for is achievable. Believe until you see the results you desire.
4. Commit and take action: Make a commitment to your goals and take action towards achieving them every day. Go all-in and take at least one step every day to move towards your goals.
5. Invest in yourself: Prioritize your personal and spiritual growth by investing in yourself first. Surround yourself with growth-minded people, hire a coach to guide you, and clean up any negative programming in your mindset that may be holding you back.

Additionally, tell everyone about your dreams and goals, as speaking them out loud can make them a reality.

Remember we get to choose in life how we are going to make an impact.

Your message has the power to change lives, and it is up to you to take it to the world, To Make Your Mark in the World.

***

To contact Rachel:

Facebook: Rachel Best

https://www.facebook.com/iamrachelbest

Instagram: @iamrachelbest

LinkedIn: Rachel Best

Websites:

Rachelbestspeaks.com

Iamrachelbest.com

Christian Rhodes

Christian Rhodes is an exceptionally talented software engineer and creative developer with over four years of experience in the technology industry. His passion for programming languages, including Python, C#, and JavaScript, is evident in his work, which spans a wide array of applications from high-quality programs to innovative game development using Unity and Unreal Engine.

Christian holds a Bachelor's Degree in Software Engineering, an AWS Cloud Practitioner Certificate, and is currently pursuing a Master's Degree in Game Design; skillset that he puts into work in his creative consulting business CR.eates LLC and CR.worlds, which specializes in immersive and imaginative experiences using web, web3, and metaverse design. Christian's tech and creative expertise has led him to author a book on Object-Oriented Programming, titled "A Creative Guide to Object-Oriented Programming." which offers a unique perspective on programming foundations. Christian is also known for his spontaneous and inventive answers in his book, often drawing examples and inspirations from TV shows, movies, and video games when explaining technical concepts to a lay audience.

Christian is also working on three additional nonfiction books in the Creative Guide series, covering AI, the Metaverse, and Cloud Computing; and is also currently working on two fiction books-- "Casey Tresor's Fairy Tale Odyssey" and "Timeless Heroes".

The Mind is Another World

By Christian Rhodes

"Are we moving? To America?"

My 10-year-old self, sat upright in the back seat of my father's 1995 BMW. I almost spilled my orange soda when I overheard my parents discussing our future - or more specifically, my future.

"Why are we moving to America?" I asked in disbelief.

"Well, Christian, it's a land of opportunity," my mother explained calmly from the passenger seat. "There are great schools, more work opportunities, and a better life for all of us."

I interjected, "A better life? You've seen the movies and TV shows, right? I don't want to move there! It's dangerous! Too many killings! What if I get shot?"

"Christian," my mother said, "it's an opportunity for you to receive the best treatment for your Sickle Cell Anemia. The medical facilities in the United States are top-notch, and we want you to have the best chance for a healthy life."

I sank back into my seat and crossed my arms in frustration. I hated the idea of being uprooted from the Ivory Coast, the only place I called home. However, my parents sacrificed a lot to come to this country for me and my brothers, so that our lives would be much better and less challenging.

I was born with a rare disease called sickle cell anemia. My parents, especially my mother, have gone through great lengths to get me the best treatment for this illness—natural remedies, supplements, prescriptions, holistic treatment and prayers—we had to travel across towns and cities, taking road trips to see several doctors and healers—anything to prevent me from having these painful Sickle Cell crisis episodes, to which my body would contort in pain as if under the grip of some unseen monster. Most of my attacks would affect my legs, limbs, back, neck, and even my head.

My labored breathing would be heard by my family, sending a chilling reminder that this cruel disease could threaten to take my life away if I was not treated quickly. Chaos and confusion would ensue whenever I ended up in a hospital. Who should be taking care of me—or at the very least, pay attention to me—amongst the busy doctors and nurses, trying to take care of many people at once.

Most of the time, the person with a sore on his back would get the treatment first. And I would be left behind screaming and crying in pain, with the thought that nobody cared about my own suffering.

Looking back, I am forever grateful that my parents have made the decision to uproot the family into the United States. It has helped me start my life over. Going back would be like taking several years of steps back. I can now consider the Ivory Coast a past life and the United States my real home. And I have my mother to thank for. Her love and sacrifice for me has led me to this very moment—me, writing this story, and having it been read by millions of people.

To the reader who is about to read my story, know that it is never too late to go after what you really want and receive what you truly desire. It all starts with what you are thinking. And over the years, I have realized that everything that has happened in my life where deliberately coming from my own personal thoughts and beliefs. Which led me to one conclusion—that the mind is another world—your inner world.

According to the Bible in Proverbs 23:7—as a man thinketh in his heart, so is he. And I have been demonstrating this subconsciously as a child. While most of the human race wants to embrace their disability as their identities, thinking that they received that injury or ailment for some blatant purpose, I was one of the few folks who cultivated a mindset that Sickle Cell Anemia was NOT a part of my identity, and it was never going to be for as long as I have breath. It was not my strength. It was not my weakness. And most importantly, it was not a part of who I am.

As of July 2015, I am officially Sickle-Cell free. I underwent a Bone Marrow Transplant, and to my great fortune, my older brother proved to be the perfect donor match, with our genetic compatibility reaching beyond an astonishing 100%.

The road to this momentous achievement was long and arduous, but I faced every challenge with unwavering perseverance, courage, and faith. As the verse in Romans 5:3-5 so aptly states, my suffering produced within me a powerful triumvirate of character traits that continue to define my life and journey in addition to an unbreakable strength - character, perseverance, and hope.

This milestone was the culmination of years of tireless effort, and a testament to the strength and resilience of the human spirit. As I continue to forge ahead on my path, I remain ever grateful for this miraculous gift of life and the incredible support of my loved ones.

Now, to embark on a new journey, playing catch-up.

As someone who went through severe sickle cell pains constantly, I have missed out on a lot of moments in my life. My disease had a profound impact on my social status and greatly impacted my life. I didn't make many friends back in middle and high school. I barely experienced teenage love—even though I had a teenage crush—and I never got to experience the college campus life. So, my way of catching up with life is to start all over by building a legacy of wealth for my family, especially my mother, who has sacrificed a lot for me.

Filled with a renewed sense of vitality and purpose, I resolved to pursue my long-held ambition of becoming a software engineer in the video gaming industry. My goal was to harness my technical prowess to facilitate and inspire other artists and developers, as I was once inspired, in the creation of the next blockbuster sensation. For me, there was no greater satisfaction than the process of building and innovating, as opposed to the mundane task of troubleshooting computer problems.

After being admitted to the Oregon Institute of Technology (OIT) on April 2016, I was eager to hit the ground running and start pursuing my passion. Over the next three years, I worked on several app projects that allowed me to develop my skills and explore different areas of interest.

One of my most notable projects was a weather application using immersive Virtual Reality. Though it was not really a game application, it used Virtual Reality, which is already a technology that serves the industry well and it was a chance to tap into that skill and its market. This app was designed to give users a more immersive experience of the weather, allowing them to feel like they were actually there. The demo for this Virtual Reality application can be found on my *YouTube* channel @christian.rhodes; and it was also part of the school's project symposium; where many people—family, friends, guests and potential employees at large companies would come and visit to check out these latest projects.

Unfortunately, something tragic happened that day. But before I go on, a little bit of background about my time at OIT.

Throughout the three consecutive years I attended the school, I was the only black student to ever attend every single one of my classes. And everyone on campus knew that about me, and my shot to prove myself worthy of their caliber, and worthy of myself and my talents, came crashing down the day of the symposium.

40 minutes before the symposium event started, my laptop crashed. Many restarting attempts did not bring the computer back into working condition. In a last-minute decision, a one-year-old computer decided it was the perfect time to malfunction. Worst, I did not back up my project and I have lost weeks of work and preparation.

So, you can imagine how I felt that day, as an African American student who always has to work twice as hard to prove himself in a country that limits their recognition and perseverance. It was a frustrating and devastating time in my life, and my lifetime chance to showcase my project at a symposium was gone forever. Looking back, it taught me the importance of always having a backup plan and never taking technology for granted. Because trust me when I say this—technology will always find a way to betray you.

After spending a week restoring every module and rewriting every code, I finally got an update on my project. Then decided to cultivate another mindset. If a neighborhood was not able to see my project, then the whole world will have to see my project. And so, I wasted no time to push it online on my YouTube channel, @christian.rhodes. Look for the video *BoreasVR*.

In June 2019, I graduated from the Oregon Institute of Technology with a degree in Software Engineering. Grateful for the opportunities that I had there and for the experiences that helped shape who I am today, I decided to transform my skills into a career.

Still passionate about video games, I started a freelancing service titled CR.eates(). A play on word with how programmers write code methods, the CR represents my first and last name. Adding the .eates next to it, I am bringing my creativity in just about anything that is on your mind. And that anything can be filled inside those empty parentheses.

On my website, createsllc.com, my strengths are on arts, tech, gaming, metaverse, stories and mindset.

At CReates LLC, my mission is to inspire and inform people about the latest advancements in technology and encourage them to explore their creativity to the fullest. I believe that anyone can be creative, regardless of their background, and I'm committed to helping people unlock their potential in this new age of innovation.

My ultimate goal is to turn CReates into a publishing agency, specializing in video games and the metaverse, which I believe is the future of the internet. Through our artistic and creative content, we hope to empower individuals to push the boundaries of what's possible and to create a better world for everyone.

As part of the CReates brand, I am working on a couple of InProg novel series, "Casey Tresor's Fairy Tale Odyssey" and "Timeless Heroes." These novels are unique in that new chapters are posted online as they're being developed for publication. Our goal is to engage with our audience in this new tech and publishing era, creating a more interactive and exciting experience for readers.

I am also developing a series of Creative Guide books, designed to teach programming and tech development using creativity. These books include "Creative Guide to Object Oriented Programming," "Creative Guide to Data Structures," and "Creative Guide to Web3 and the Metaverse." My aim is to help those who have a passion for programming but think more like an artist than a scientist. I am also looking to expand my horizons, and plan to launch some video game installments in the near future.

My time at OIT, along with my perseverance through Sickle Cell Anemia, has shaped me into the person I am today. I'm proud to say that it's never too late to follow your dreams, and I'm excited to help others achieve theirs through the work we're doing at CReates. But as always, it should start with their mindset.

My journey has been filled with adversity, but I have learned to overcome it. I have gone through the pain and the fear of Sickle Cell Anemia, the challenges of moving to a new country, and the disappointment of technology failing me at critical moments. But through it all, I have learned to never give up, to always keep pushing forward, and to believe in myself and my abilities.

I have also learned of two very valuable key points in all of this— the storyteller is the most powerful person on the planet; and your mind is another world. Now what does that mean and what does that have to do with my story?

Stories have the power to change people's lives, to inspire them, and to push them to achieve their goals. Stories can create empathy, and they can help people see the world in a different way. Through storytelling, people can share their experiences and connect with others on a deeper level. And I believe that if we can harness the power of storytelling, we can create a better world for all.

But do also acknowledge that our minds are another world. Our thoughts and beliefs shape our reality, and we have the power to create our own world within our minds through storytelling, giving inspirations for others to create their own realities. Our mindset can determine our success or failure, and it can influence how we see the world around us. We have the power to control our thoughts and beliefs, and that we can use this power to achieve our goals and create the life we always wanted.

The relationship between storytelling, our mind, and mindset is that they are all connected. Storytelling can influence our thoughts and beliefs, which in turn can shape our mindset. If we hear stories that inspire us, we are more likely to believe that we can achieve our goals. If we tell ourselves stories about our own abilities and potential, we are more likely to have a growth mindset and to push ourselves to achieve more.

My own journey is a testament to the power of storytelling and mindset. Despite facing numerous challenges and setbacks, I never gave up on my dreams and I never took my illness as part of my identity.

Your mind is another world. and within that world, every goal and every path you set for yourself, get to it, see yourself completing it first within, and see to it that it is completed in your reality.

***

To contact Christian:

My Linktree -

https://linktr.ee/christianrhodes

Nonfiction book - Creative Guide to Object Oriented Programming

https://www.blurb.com/bookstore/invited/9874318/ff27965df33d8 d7d191f668863b493469efc2bc6

InProg fiction book - Casey Tresor's Fairy Tale Odyssey Book 1 - The Book of Wonders

https://www.caseytresor.com/

InProg nonfiction book - Prompt Wizardry -

https://www.crworlds.com/

Dr. Karen Kramer

Dr. Karen Kramer is a guiding light who has transformed the lives of countless individuals around the globe for over three decades.

With a profound understanding of the human mind and a specialty in grief recovery, Dr. Karen's true passion lies in helping individuals navigate heart-wrenching experiences such as divorce, loss of loved ones, and traumatic events.

Corporations and nonprofits (including United Way, American Express, Nike, Boeing, and Google) have sought Dr. Karen's invaluable counsel. Her expertise also embraces entrepreneurs, beauty pageant titleholders, actresses, stay-at-home moms, and retirees.

As a faculty member, program manager, and executive coach at the prestigious Center for Creative Leadership, Dr. Karen guided leaders from new managers to C-suite executives. She also served as a co-facilitator and program director for Teen Wisdom Inc., certifying teenage girl life coaches. As the Head Coach for Recalibrate360, Dr. Karen played a pivotal role in certifying individuals in Neuro-Linguistics Programming (NLP), Time Line Therapy®, and Hypnotherapy.

In 2022, Dr. Karen unveiled the awe-inspiring VillaVision Wellness & Retreat Center – a sanctuary of tranquility, nestled in sun-drenched Southern California. Here, women can discover profound happiness, rejuvenating health, and inner wholeness – a testament to uplifting lives from within.

As a woman-preneur and a mother who successfully raised five children in a blended family, she intimately understands the art of juggling life's priorities while maintaining a semblance of sanity.

Good Grief! - Death, Divorce & Other Losses

By Dr. Karen Kramer

"Don't sacrifice the beauties of tomorrow by focusing on the sorrows of yesterdays."

~ Dr. Karen Kramer

Where were you on the day of 9/11?

If you were born before 1995 and had access to the news, it's likely that pieces of that day – September 11, 2001 – are etched vividly in your memory. I recall arriving early at work that Tuesday morning, an hour before the start of our five-day leadership development program. The atmosphere in the office felt eerie. As I walked through the open cubicles, I noticed a coworker intently watching a TV at his desk. Curiosity piqued; I glanced over just in time to witness a plane crash into one of the Twin Towers.

I stood frozen. Even though it seemed like a poorly made movie, the screams near the reporter and the flashing news ticker made it painfully real.

That day marked a profound shift from what was considered normal. The meticulously planned leadership program had to be set aside as my co-facilitator and I swiftly adjusted our focus to manage and support the emotional well-being of the participants that morning. The rest of the agenda had to wait.

**

Change, while uncomfortable, presents an opportunity for transformation and growth. Grief is change. It cannot be simply overcome; it needs to be integrated into our lives to facilitate forward movement. By normalizing conversations about grief experienced during life-altering changes, we can support healthy processing and empower ourselves and others to move forward in life.

Just recently, within a span of 24 hours, three separate friends reached out for advice on grief support. They knew I had dealt with similar grief experiences firsthand and had helped others navigate life's challenges. Let's face it, unexpected hurdles come our way, and one of the most universal experiences is the loss of a loved one. Spoiler alert: death is inevitable, and avoiding this topic won't prevent it from happening.

In this chapter you will explore simple and memorable frameworks for coping strategies, facilitating conversations about common life experiences, including the loss of loved ones and pets, break-ups, job transitions, relocations, academic changes, becoming empty nesters, retirement, health declines and diagnoses, accidents, financial setbacks, and more.

Let us define **grief** here as, "*the deep emotional sorrow and the process of coping after a traumatic event when what once was is no longer.*"

Clutching onto the life we once had can be harmful, leading to sadness, frustration, disappointment, anger, and a host of other emotions. Various models have been used to support the grief process. The following are two I've used in the past with leadership and corporate clients, and then we will move into a model I created to support my clients as they actively grieve personal life-altering scenarios.

Proven Methods for Corporate Change

Throughout my work at the Center for Creative Leadership since 1993, I have guided individuals ranging from new managers to C-suite executives through various organizational changes including merges and layoffs. The following two models are popularly known in the field of leadership in helping leaders successfully move through challenging times.

The Logical Model

One leadership model is the Bridges Transition Model (BTM), developed by William Bridges and introduced in his 1991 book *Managing Transitions: Making the Most of Change*. This model provides valuable insights for individuals and organizations, helping them navigate the personal and human aspects of change.

BTM highlights the distinct phases individuals experience during periods of transition that result from change. BTM differentiates between *change*, an external event that happens to you, and *transition*, an internal process that unfolds as a result of the change event. It encompasses the psychological journey within your mind as you internalize and adapt to the new circumstances brought about by the change.

Here is a brief explanation of the three stages of managing transitions:

Stage 1 - Ending & Letting Go: Transition begins with the change event, the conclusion of something familiar. In this phase, individuals confront their losses and acquire the skills to navigate through them.

Stage 2 - Neutral Zone: After letting go of the past, you enter a period of uncertainty known as the neutral zone. The old has faded away, and the new is not yet fully established.

Stage 3 - New Beginnings: The final stage involves cultivating new insights, values, and attitudes. It represents a surge of energy directed towards a fresh path and serves as a manifestation of a revitalized identity.

The Emotional Model

To simplify and enhance understanding, I have often utilized the SARAH model, a known model in the business world, with corporate clients as a practical framework for navigating unsettling news and guiding individuals through transitions. It is loosely based on a 5-stage model of grief by Dr. Elizabeth Kübler-Ross, a Swiss-American psychiatrist.

The grieving process is a deeply personal journey, yet it often follows a similar flow. SARAH is an easy-to-remember model that can assist both yourself and others through the most predictable emotional patterns of responses people may go through during the grief period of transition.

Here is a brief overview of those emotional patterns:

Shock: The initial response can range from intense emotions to a numbing absence of feelings. Others may struggle to comprehend the magnitude of the change, and individuals may deny its reality out of fear. Other word associations are *sadness* or *surprise*.

Anger: As the shock subsides, feelings of anger or anxiety may arise as individuals come to understand the implications of the change and experience a sense of loss. Another word association is *anxiety*.

Resistance: During this phase, individuals resist and reject the need for change. They may find reasons to support their resistance and display apathy, detachment, or a temporary loss of hope. Other word associations are *rejection, rage, rebellion, reactive,* and *"rock bottom."*

Acceptance: Gradually, individuals come to terms with the change and embrace its reality. They recognize the benefits and positive aspects of the new circumstances. Another word association is *action*.

Healing: This stage marks a pivotal moment when individuals actively seek help and support. It signifies their readiness to work towards healing and moving forward. Other associated words are *hope, help,* and *happiness.*

Now, let us delve into the transformative actions and possibilities that lie ahead as we embark on a journey of healing, resilience, and rebuilding, using a simplified framework that incorporates the previous two models.

Putting it Together Into GRIEF

In 2012, while grieving my father's passing, I was confronted with yet another devastating loss just three months later – my son's father's unexpected departure from this world.

I found myself in uncharted territory, grappling with the daunting task of explaining to my then nine-year-old son that he would no longer have the opportunity to see his father. I sat my son down on the bed, my voice trembling, and spoke words that flowed from the depths of my sorrow. The details of that day remain shrouded in a haze of emotions, leaving only fragmented memories in their wake.

What remains vivid in my mind, however, is the hauntingly blank expression on my son's face – an outward reflection of the internal turmoil he was experiencing. It was evident that he had entered the first stage of SARAH – shock. At his tender age of nine, he lacked the cognitive capacity, coping mechanisms, and life experiences necessary to navigate such a profound and sudden change.

Simultaneously, he found himself thrust into the initial stage of BTM. The routines he had grown accustomed to, such as his father picking him up after school on scheduled days and their shared outings together, were abruptly extinguished, forever altering the landscape of his familiar world. The foundations of his reality had crumbled, and what once provided stability and comfort was now a distant memory.

**

Based on my research and work with clients, I created the GRIEF model, an acronym that encapsulates the essence of grief and serves as a guide for navigating various life events. This framework applies to any form of change, from helping children through the loss of a parent to the COVID-19 pandemic, career shifts, financial changes, educational advancements, relocation, marriage, or divorce. This framework may apply to your personal experience, or you may use it to support others through life-altering changes.

The GRIEF model consists of five distinct phases to help someone process: **Gather, Relate, Involve, Ease,** and **Focus**. It integrates the concepts of SARAH and BTM, providing a comprehensive approach to understanding and healing. It is a graceful approach to supporting the process and our emotions as it focuses on communication and sharing experiences. It helps soften the experience, bring comfort to those involved, and gives grace to the highs and lows of the grief journey. It adapts to flow with the organic experience you may have during times of change.

Gather

The initial step in the grieving process is represented by the letter G, which stands for **Gather**. This phase involves *collecting and exchanging information about the recent change event*. Think of it as the rational, intellectual aspect of the GRIEF process, engaging the *logical mind*.

This phase corresponds to BTM's *Ending* (Stage 1). It involves reflecting on the past, acknowledging losses, and processing information about the change.

During this phase, communication is important. Share relevant facts and tailor the information to the recipient, especially so children fully understand and avoid overwhelm.

Relate

The second letter in the process is R, representing **Relate**, which involves *actively listening to others' thoughts and feelings while also acknowledging your own*. This aspect forms the *emotional* core of the GRIEF process.

Transitioning from the *Ending* to the *Neutral Zone* brings psychological readjustments and uncertainty. Motivation for daily tasks may decrease, while negative emotions may increase. Most notable emotions experienced during this phase of the grief process are *shock, sadness, anger, anxiety,* and *resistance* representing the first three phases of **SARAH**.

Engage in conversations about feelings and the implications of the change. Observe their thoughts, emotions, actions, and reactions to understand the impact of the change. Listen and take the time to truly hear and empathize with them. Introduce the concept of SARAH as a framework for discussing and recognizing their own and others' emotional stages without judgment. Here's how to navigate them.

Shock, sadness, and *anxiety* are marked by intense feelings or numbness. Be present, listen attentively, and empathize without judgment. Honor emotions and ask open-ended questions. Creating a safe space for expression.

Anger is a natural response to loss. Resist the urge to fight anger with more anger. Show empathy and allow others to express their anger. Communicate your points only after validating another's emotions. Encourage healthy outlets like exercise, safe venting, or therapy.

In *resistance*, individuals reject change and may deflect by focusing on other issues. They use logic and reasoning as a defense mechanism. Practice patience and attentive listening. Set appropriate boundaries and recognize these behaviors as protective shields against discomfort and loss.

Expressing and validating emotions is crucial to navigate the grieving process and embrace change. Regularly revisit and monitor individuals' progress through grief phases, respecting their unique journeys.

Involve

The third letter in the process is I, which stands for **Involve** *others in the process of finding solutions*. Think of this step as the *action-oriented* aspect of the GRIEF process.

The *Neutral Zone* (BTM Stage 2) shifts the focus towards finding a new way of life beyond what-once-was. This crucial time forms the essence of the transition process between the former reality and the emerging new one creating an opportunity for creativity and renewal.

Engage others in practical tasks, respecting their needs and preferences; encourage open communication, support, and collaborative decision-making to foster unity and forward momentum. Embracing the new may not be immediate, even after letting go of the old.

During this stage, individuals may still *resist* change. Patience is crucial. Develop action plans with clear time frames and success indicators. Encourage small, achievable steps. Support goals, celebrate wins, and tackle easily attainable tasks first.

By involving others emotionally, we progress from *resistance* to *acceptance,* embracing change and finding hope for the new chapter. Active participation brings purpose, empowerment, and contributes to healing and growth.

The *acceptance* stage is a milestone in the grieving process. Individuals begin to embrace the new reality and recognize its benefits. Acceptance doesn't mean being okay with the loss, but rather adjusting to a changed life. Acceptance also doesn't end grief; it's a series of smaller moments over time. These moments include tasks like planning and attending change-related events (such as a funeral), signifying progress in the acceptance journey.

Ease

The fourth letter in the GRIEF process is E, representing **Ease** *with the support of professional help*. Think of this stage as the *supportive hands* that guide you through grief.

This is the transition from the *Neutral Zone* to the *New Beginning*. Even if you've accepted the changes, there will be confusion, uncertainty, and impatience. Expressing your feelings is crucial. You won't have all the answers at the start.

Seeking help aids the *healing* journey. Signs of progress include increased energy, motivation, engagement, and being open to support. Witness a notable change, upliftment, and renewed determination.

To support individuals through grief, educate them about what you learned on your journey and share coping strategies. Discuss healthy ways to cope, seek support from friends or professionals, and consider legal or therapeutic help, if needed. Reach out before reaching "rock bottom" and involve your support network. Advocate for your own care and remember that healing involves acceptance, integration, and moving forward.

In cases of prolonged grief, seek professional help. Prolonged grief disorder was added to the Diagnostic and Statistical Manual of Mental Disorders in 2022. Seeking appropriate support becomes crucial in such cases. Profound traumas require professional support to heal effectively.

It's important to recognize that fully comprehending the depth of the pain and disbelief over a life-altering event, and processing the experience cannot be rushed. Grief work is not about reaching a point where all pain disappears but rather developing the ability to remember the change (or life before it) with more positive feelings than painful. Healing occurs as acceptance deepens, allowing individuals to integrate their loss into their lives and move forward.

Focus

The final letter in the GRIEF process is F, which stands for **Focus** *on the next chapter in life and celebrate when achieved*. Think of this as the stage where you gain clarity of *vision* within the grief journey.

The *New Beginning* stage represents a surge of energy towards a revitalized identity and a new path. Skillful navigation of transitions empowers individuals to embrace fresh roles, find purpose, and make impactful contributions. This stage brings a profound reorientation and personal renewal.

This phase also marks the unique start of one's own purposeful and value-aligned life. Acceptance and newfound energy propel you forward as you shape this new reality. Define your "new normal," envision your goals and values, and experiment to find what works best. Seek assistance when needed and celebrate small victories along the way. Coach and support others in setting goals, fostering discussion, and finding balance. Embrace celebration and collective progress as you create new traditions and purpose together.

** **

The GRIEF model also emerged from both my successes and failures in supporting my son through grief, including my own experiences. Little did I know, as I laid on my bed with my nine-year-old in shock on that mid-October evening, that our lives would be forever changed. What once was, was no longer.

As an introvert, my son didn't openly express his feelings, and I mistakenly assumed his silence meant he was okay. How wrong I was!

A year later, he began experiencing stomach problems. For seven long years, we sought medical, dietary, and psychological help (which he resisted) to alleviate his pain. Meanwhile, I watched helplessly as his once-bright spirit, beloved by peers, talent in water polo, and on the path to becoming an Eagle Scout, faded away. Sports, extracurricular activities, academics, and his social network all suffered. I was losing my son!

It wasn't until he turned 17 that I discovered the techniques to unlock the hidden grief within him and reignite his spirit, enabling him to become the thriving young adult he is today, now approaching 21.

In honor of my son, his struggles, and my own past regrets and "should'ves," I offer this framework. It opens the doors of communication by gathering information, fosters connections by regularly checking in and monitoring individuals' progress through their emotions, involves them in the process, seeks support to ease the pain, and encourages a healthy focus on embracing the "new normal."

In Summary

"When you come from a place of curiosity, you open yourself up to possibilities."

~Dr. Karen Kramer

Grief is a deeply personal experience that varies from person to person, shaped by our unique circumstances and relationships. By openly expressing our experience of moving through grief, and supporting others by actively listening to their experience, we can have a meaningful dialogue on grief and introduce the practical GRIEF framework for navigating life's challenges.

Change may be uncomfortable, but it also offers opportunities for transformation and growth. Grief cannot be simply overcome; it must be integrated into our lives for forward progress. By embracing healthy coping strategies, we fortify our emotional resilience and overcome setbacks.

Our response to life's challenges shapes our journey of healing and growth. Navigating grief can empower us to let go, move forward, and embrace the life we desire. Alternatively, it can trap us in repetitive patterns, hindering our aspirations. However, there is always hope. By taking steps, making choices, and exploring new paths, we can create the life we truly want.

***

To contact Dr. Karen:

Email: DrKaren@TheVillaVision.com

Website: www.DrKarenKramer.com

Website: www.TheVillaVision.com

Facebook / Instagram / LinkedIn: @DrKarenKramer

This chapter is adapted from the forthcoming book "Good Grief: Death, Divorce, and Other Losses" by Dr. Karen Kramer (anticipated release date: Fall 2023).

For one-on-one coaching or speaking opportunities, book a call at www.DrKarenKramer.com.

Michael Cupo

My name is Michael Cupo, I was born in Newark NJ on August 8, 1958. For reasons unbeknownst to me I always felt like something was missing in my life. Although I had every opportunity a person could want, I always made decisions that weren't conducive to my well-being. I started using alcohol, drugs, and gambling at the age of thirteen and this continued until June of 1987. In the next four years I got married, bought a house, and had two children. By society's standards my life was a success, but something was still missing that didn't allow me to enjoy life. I have since come to understand what this something is. My struggles with life were all self inflicted, mainly because of a Conditioned Mind view that blocked my ability to give love. This is what led me to the writing of my book "*It's Monday Only in Your Mind: You Are Not Your Thoughts.*" What I now understand is nothing new, but it's unique in the way that I see it. What I see is so practical that anyone who thinks they're not getting the most out of their life will be able to understand why. I have since found the peace I always sought, and I have come to understand that it was always there, I just didn't know it.

Inner Awakening

By Michael Cupo

A Brief Summary:

My name is Michael Cupo. I'm 64 years old and here to write about my life to help others understand their own life. As far back as I can remember, I have always wanted things to be different in my life. Life was always very confusing to me. I started drinking at age 13, which seemed to solve many of my problems – but it was only a mask.

In 1987 I stopped drinking, and that's when my problems really started. Although life on the material plane got much better, I never understood the change needed to occur had to come from within. I experienced the same feelings before I started using alcohol as a solution to my problems; I just reached for other things as a substitute for alcohol. This caused needless suffering to me and others until the age of 49.

After all those years of suffering, I asked myself, "What made me think something outside myself was going to make me happy?" So, I set out to investigate this, which led to the writing of my book "It's Monday Only in Your Mind: You Are Not Your Thoughts." What I learned and wrote about doesn't involve any specific religion or philosophy. It's all about how a person's inner & outside influences create Conditioned Mind Patterns. These Mind Patterns are based on self-centeredness and block our own innate goodness, which is based in love, from being the default setting of our mind.

I learned how these Mind Patterns were the cause of my problems. Until I understood this and learned not to allow them to control me, life wouldn't change. I would continue to be controlled by them as if I were a puppet on a string.

My book is an Inspirational Memoir of Recovery from the I Self, my ego. My passion is to share my story and solution with anyone who wants to change the way they view life. I aspire to spare others the pain and suffering I have endured & caused.

The changes that occurred in me are real, but they didn't happen because I am special — they occurred because the veil of ignorance has been removed. In fact, I found I didn't have to change my lifestyle as much as change the way I was attached to that lifestyle.

I've been at the same job for 34 years. I've been married for 31 years and have two children. I own a home and drive a new car. It would appear I had everything I needed to be happy, but this wasn't the case.

Worldly possessions are to be enjoyed, but only with the awareness they're not who we are, that they will have to be let go of one day — whether we want to or not. You can do whatever is in your heart to do; understand the more you think those things will bring you the fulfillment you so desire, the more that fulfillment will elude you. You're complete just the way you are; you just don't know it.

Discovering Love Within:

I'm here to share with you how a profound change in my view of life led to the opening of my heart. I have given much thought concerning the message I'm sharing here. What some of my experiences have afforded me is to see that life is one continuous journey, which is always occurring Now. I didn't always view life in this way. Because of how my mind was conditioned, I always looked beyond the Now to the past or future for what was considered a better place to be. My mind had been conditioned to believe that I needed to be somewhere other than Now, but Now is where life happens regardless of what's going on.

This isn't easy to comprehend but understand when you're wishing for what's happening right now to be different, you're wishing your life away. This is something that needs to be realized if you're going to truly live life to the fullest and not wait for it to be the way you think it should be. When you understand this, your inner struggles will lessen because you'll know you're complete just the way you are. Here is a favorite saying of mine: "Live each day as if it will be your last because one day you will be right."

There are many different roads to choose from in life. I know I've made many mistakes trying to find the right one. I'm not here to tell anyone which road to take, as everyone will make their own mistakes. But I will tell you this, over the course of my life, I always looked outside myself for my answers, and even when it seemed I found them, it was never lasting. This was not the fault of anyone; it was just the view of life I developed. This developed view created an absence or void in my life; I equate this to a lack of self-love. This is what was lacking in the decision-making process of my life. Every decision I made had only my own self-absorbed interest at heart, and it was always based on being a benefit only to me. This is what led to my struggles and discontentment.

By having the direction of my decisions based on satisfying myself, regardless of how things worked out, I was always looking for the next satisfaction. When I experienced my shift, it was the first time I had an awareness of this, and I was able to say, enough. All my years of confusion were understood in this simple yet profound realization. This was when I came to understand that at the center of all my confusion was the unawareness of an inner loving energy in my life. This energy can be called God, but it's not so much something out there as it's the energy of the love within my heart. This absence led to my inner discontentment and struggles and why I was being led around like a puppet on a string.

I didn't know this inner discontentment or absence of love was even there; I just knew I was never happy with how things were. It wasn't taught to me that love is the true base of existence; without it, inner discontentment and struggles never go away, no matter what's reached for to try and fill life. Even with life seemingly precisely as wanted, without love, there will always be reaching for the next fix because there will always be discontentment. I know now love is the only thing that'll bring the fulfillment of my inner desires. Today I know I can do anything I want to do, but if love isn't at the base of my decisions, it will be challenging to sustain a continuous sense of fulfillment no matter what is accomplished.

My life today is a direct result of mediation, disciplining an undisciplined mind. This is helping me understand how to stop allowing the merry-go-round mind from controlling my life; it's not magic. It takes a willingness to change because of the way the mind becomes conditioned. Identifying self-absorbing Conditioned Mind Patterns and changing them, so life is based in love is what's been revealed to me. I have developed the Four Principles of the Conditioned Mind to show how the Conditioned Mind can be changed once you become aware it needs changing. This is strong language because it goes against what's taught in society, but before it's discounted, look and see if you're truly in control of your mind and getting all you can out of life. If you aren't, you're the only one who can change it.

There's a reason the world's in the condition it's in. We all need to pull together to become aware of this and share the love in our hearts. We are the change the world needs, but it will only occur when it's understood that our love for others has to come first. Everyone has the responsibility to make the world a better place by looking at the energy that's in control of their life. If it's self-absorbing energy, it will not benefit anyone, but if it's love-absorbing energy, it will benefit our entire human family. After all, it's the world we all share.

This is not some magical path for a select few, it's open to anyone, but it takes much practice and discipline not to be controlled by a Conditioned Mind. Everyone has their own journey in life and will find the path they think is best, but how about this, what if a path is chosen as what's best for others? Wouldn't that be different; this is the difference that needs to occur if our world is to change.

The Journey:

Did you ever wonder what goes through the mind of someone immersed in their self-absorbed thoughts? I can tell you in detail as I spent years living unconsciously — suffering and causing others to suffer.

Did you ever see someone scream at a stranger in public? Did you ever see a drunk or an addict passed out in a doorway? And more honestly, were you ever that screaming person or that over-intoxicated person? Did you ever do something completely crazy without understanding why?

I've been there — big time — and I've stopped being there.

In this chapter, I share my journey of a profound change and discovery of a different way of viewing life. I also share this in greater detail in my book "It's Monday Only in Your Mind: You Are Not Your Thoughts."

What I have written here is not just about controlling reckless behavior and addictions. This article is about living from a new place, a beautiful and peaceful place. It's about going somewhere I never expected to be. No, I didn't leave home; I didn't leave my wife, my job, or my family. I left my self-absorbed behavior behind.

It was never my intention to share in this way, but the more I talked to people about the changes in my life, the more interested they became in how those changes came about. Many said that my account "made sense" to them; they just "never thought about it in the way I described," so I sensed a need to share what was revealed.

The things I write about are to be used as pointers to assist in life's journey. I share my experience so I might touch someone who feels as frustrated and confused about life as I did. It's not my purpose to save or change anyone. I write so others can read about my experiences and look within to discover their own path.

Please don't feel judged as to whether you're living right or wrong. Rather, based on my own insights, I hope to cast a light on why we do what we do. I will explain how influences, which I call Conditioned Mind Patterns, cause our reactions and dictate our behavior. When I write about these patterns, caps are used because I feel they have become so ingrained in our private and collective lives and have assumed an unwarranted prominence.

In the Four Principles of the Conditioned Mind below, I describe how Conditioned Mind Patterns are formed and how they influence what we think, say, do, and feel. I reveal how they control our lives but can be changed — if you *truly* want to change them.

We don't react randomly to life circumstances; we behave as we've been conditioned. Every day we come upon situations that bring us to a spiritual fork in the road. When this occurs, we have a choice that either puts us in harmony or out of harmony with life. Many of us are not aware we have this choice. We think there is only one way to go: the default way we have been conditioned to go. We take that route again and again. This is just what we do until something happens, which allows us to see another way.

We're deeply habituated by what we know and can't seem to let go of our familiar ways. We see other options but still, go where our conditioning leads us. Then one day, we stop, and for whatever reason, we take the other route. We learn it offers greater benefits, and we never want to go the old way again. We will go the familiar way again because that's the nature of a Conditioned Mind. But a new awareness has entered our being, which starts us on a new road that will lead us to love ourselves and, in the process, love all beings.

This awareness can be called a spiritual awakening, but I'm not a certified religious trainer, clergyman, or psychologist. I don't profess to be an expert on any of this; I strictly share my experience. I'm only one person coming to understand his own mind and life. I simply share my discoveries. I have embarked on a journey to investigate why I've acted as I did without regard for consequences. I had everything a person could want, and I wasn't happy. I've been led to an answer that has allowed me to see things differently and become happy, joyous, and free.

Learning to live this new way will not happen without cooperation. The old way tries to draw you back because that's what's known. But when you start the discovery about the Conditioned Mind Patterns and how to quiet them, the reaching ceases for those old, fixed solutions. As the mind becomes quieter through a steady practice of meditation, there's more awareness of these Conditioned Mind Patterns. As we become more aware of the conditioning, we can then choose to change our Mind Patterns to live in cooperation and harmony with life. This harmony is what allows us to bring joy, peace, and happiness into our lives and, thus, into the lives of others.

Once these changes start occurring, our behavior changes. We have a new choice of responding to others from a place of love. We'll probably have this choice for the first time in our lives. By learning to quiet our minds through the discipline of meditation, what we're really learning is to open our hearts. The more our heart is opened, the less our life is controlled by our Conditioned Thinking and the more guided we are by love.

The Four Principles of the Conditioned Mind:

If there isn't a process in place to understand why one thinks, says, and does what they do, what's done will continue to happen randomly, and life will be lived as if it's a game of chance.

1. The Principle of a Conditioned Mind - Understanding.

This is the cornerstone of all the other principles because without understanding your conditioning, you will never know what you're truly up against, and the Conditioned Mind will remain in control of your life. This conditioning is subtle; it's present even if it appears your life is outwardly perfect. The moment you think about something, you can be sure it arises from a Conditioned Mind Pattern. How do I know this? Because a thought that arises wouldn't do so without the conditioning being in place, original thoughts are rare indeed. Understanding the Conditioned Mind is the beginning of becoming aware of your thoughts and what you can do to stop being controlled by them.

2. The Principle of What Causes the Conditioning - Attachment

Once there's an understanding of Principle One, the next Principal addresses what embeds the Conditioned Mind Pattern into one's subconscious. This occurs because of attachment, which is to one's I Self, as it's described in my book. It's this story of "I" that one has been creating their entire existence, and it's where all attachment arises from. Pure and simple, if one didn't create this I Self, there would be nobody to attach to a thought.

3. The Principle of Awareness of the Conditioning - Realizing

So now there's a deeper understanding of why one thinks, says, and does what they do. What happens in Principle Three is there's the realization of one's behavior, and it's seen how so many times one has acted in ways that weren't beneficial to themselves or anyone else. In this realization, there's finally a choice that for years wasn't there. Life occurs, and the conditioning arises, but now it's understood, so there's no attachment to what arises. Although the mind will try, it's through this realization that allows one to see it's your own mind that's telling you to act in ways that aren't beneficial to yourself or anyone else.

4. The Principle of Conditioned Mind Freedom - Practice

Principle Four is the glue that holds the process of these principles together. These Four Principles allow something tangible to be held onto, so one sees how putting a practice in place allows the mind to settle. The more one practices, the more the mind settles; with a settled mind, there's much more awareness of the first three principles. And with more awareness of the first three principles, the mind settles more. This goes round and round, and as it does, these principles feed off each other as the mind naturally aligns with its true nature of stillness.

It's written in the bible to "Be Still" it doesn't say to read another book, get a spouse, a degree, a better job, and so on. Not that there's anything wrong with any of these things, but it's in a practice that anchors you in the present moment which develops the discipline necessary for these principles to take hold. If the time comes for deeper self-investigation to expose the lies of the Conditioned Mind even further, my book could be the next step in the process of breaking the hold of one's Conditioned Mind.

***

To contact Michael:

www.mondayinyourmind.com

http://michaelcupo40.wordpress.com/

https://www.facebook.com/groups/itsmondayinyourmind/

Cheryl Elizabeth Williams

Cheryl Elizabeth Williams, an Executive Director, Public Speaker, and Life Coach, has effectively mentored numerous individuals towards success, firmly believing in their potential to thrive in the face of adversity. According to her, the formation of diamonds in each one of us is only possible through intense pressure and hardships.

Cheryl's childhood was marked by abuse, neglect, and homelessness before she reached the age of 18. However, she refused to allow her unfortunate circumstances to define her. Despite growing up in a poverty-stricken neighborhood in Chicago, she has emerged as a successful businesswoman, a devoted mother to two children, and a reigning Queen in the USA Ambassador pageant. In addition, she manages a non-profit organization that provides educational assistance to those in the foster care system. She has a deep compassion for children who have experienced painful or difficult circumstances, and she works tirelessly to raise awareness and funds to increase empathy for foster kids, spreading love and compassion in the world.

Possessing Billion-dollar Vibes

By Cheryl Elizabeth Williams

Billion Dollar Vibes

The world of entrepreneurship is a fascinating and competitive one. It is a world where ideas are transformed into reality, and where the most innovative thinkers are able to create businesses that change the way we live and work. In this world, there are a few individuals who possess what can only be described as "billion-dollar vibes." These are the people who seem to have a sixth sense when it comes to spotting the next big thing. They have an innate ability to identify opportunities and create products or services that not only meet a need, but also capture the imagination of the masses.

The story of billion-dollar vibes is one of passion, hard work, and vision. It is the story of individuals who are able to see beyond the present and into the future, and who have the tenacity to pursue their dreams relentlessly. These individuals are not afraid to take risks, and they are not afraid to fail. They know that every failure is a steppingstone to success, and they use these failures to learn and grow.

One of the most inspiring examples of billion-dollar vibes is the story of Elon Musk. The founder of SpaceX, Tesla, and The Boring Company, Musk is a true visionary who has been able to turn his ideas into reality. His passion for space travel led him to create SpaceX, a company that has revolutionized the space industry. His vision for sustainable energy led him to create Tesla, a company that is changing the way we think about cars and energy. And his desire to alleviate traffic congestion led him to create The Boring Company, a company that is developing innovative solutions to transportation.

But Elon Musk is not the only example of billion-dollar vibes. There are countless others who have been able to achieve success through their passion and vision.

It's time for you to make your own mark, create wealth, and bring real-world solutions to current problems! Imagine yourself as a billionaire. Where would you live? Where would you travel to? Most importantly, how many people would you help with that money? What population are you passionate about helping, and what's the biggest problem you have a passion for solving? What gifts do you have, and how can you benefit the world in a way that AI can never do?

The motivation to create wealth is called drive, and it's important. But to make copious amounts of money, you can't just dream up how you would be a consumer of large amounts of money. Creating wealth is not all about mindset; it's about what gifts you have and how you can benefit the world in unique ways.

Imagine what your billionaire self would be like. What does your billionaire self-VIBE like? What does being in your billionaire presence make you feel like? What do you eat? What fashions do you dress yourself in? What do you smell like? What grooming would you do to feel like a billionaire? How do people treat you? What kind of sway do you have to your walk? What does it FEEL like to be you? What skills do you have? What do you talk to others about through your conversational skills? What jokes would you tell to make others feel comfortable and happy around you? What charm do you possess? How do you spend your time? Are you helping the homeless build career skill sets? What authority and expertise have you established? How proud of yourself, you must be, to be a self-made billionaire? You are adding value to the table in a world that is being taken over by robots performing surgery and 3D printers building houses within three days!

Presenting yourself in a way that if you were seated among the Marc Cubans of the world, you would fit in, but with your own unique persona. Having billionaire vibes means you are adding trillion-dollar value to the world with your intellect!

In your billionaire vibe visualization, do you feel enough? Do you feel skilled? Do you feel healed of all health problems? Is your house organized? Are you feeling sexy? Are you eating your fresh fruits and veggies with a smile on your face? Do you have a massive exercise room? Do you feel loved and increasingly happy and energetic? Are you well prepared for the future?

As a billionaire, how would you handle someone not treating you with respect? You wouldn't let it get you down! You're too blessed to be stressed! You're living out your true-life mission of helping and kingdom leadership!

Women empowerment doesn't come easy. How do you go from being underpaid and undervalued to being a Queen that is an authority figure in the world? It doesn't happen on accident! Surround yourself with high vibrational people and if you're not feeling as confident as the confidence they give off, increase your vibration! You belong in the wide ocean, but if you don't feel comfortable interacting with dolphins and sharks yet, work up to it. Grow from the inside out. Have so much personality and joy within you that talent scouts scout you at the mall!

Always remember your billionaire vibes self. You are the greatest creator and visionary that you've ever met in your life! For more life coaching tips and advice on living your happiest and most prepared life, email me at williams.cheryl.elizabeth@gmail.com.

I say the following with great humility. It doesn't matter that I've been featured as a woman entrepreneur in Forbes magazine. It doesn't matter that I'm a Queen who attracts wealthy sponsors. What matters to me is that I truly am helping people create the life they have only dreamed about, no matter what family they were born into. The following are true testimonials of the impact I've been making in my community as a life coach.

Testimonials about Cheryl Elizabeth Williams

> - Cheryl's life coaching is a transformational experience where she helps individuals overcome their traumas and turn their dreams into reality. Her approach stems from the belief that we are the masters of our own happiness and can assertively create the life we want. She inspires her clients to stay the course of living out their dreams until their last breath, emphasizing that the skills needed for success can be learned along the way. With Cheryl as their guide, people are empowered to achieve their goals, break free from limiting beliefs, and take control of their lives. - Lisa

- Williams' coaching is not just a remedy for trauma; it's a ticket to achieving your aspirations, no matter how challenging your circumstances. "Don't settle for whatever fate you were born with. Her life is a testament to the fact that you can overcome any obstacle and make your dreams come true." - Jill

- Cheryl possesses a rare spirit and redefines what true strength is. Despite experiencing heartbreak and abuse, Cheryl confronts the evils of the world with a smile and embarks on every day as a new opportunity to explore. Cheryl utilizes her light to restore, piece by piece, day by day, and is a selfless spiritual warrior and bastion of hope. - Pryce

- Why hire Cheryl as your life coach? For me, it's Cheryl's trustworthiness and ability to make me feel comfortable and understood. Cheryl helps me with courage, helps me feel better about myself, and corrects my upbringing. I was raised by a neglectful adopted mom. Cheryl is like a mom to me. She makes me feel loved, informed, and empowered. - Bradley

- If you're feeling stuck, unhappy, or held back by trauma, a life coach like Cheryl Elizabeth Williams can help. With her guidance, you can reframe negative thoughts, develop a sense of self-esteem and purpose, and achieve your dreams. Don't let trauma hold you back. With the help of a life coach like Cheryl Elizabeth Williams, you can overcome the past, achieve your goals, and live a fulfilling life. - George

Giving Foster Youth Aging Out of the Foster Care System Billion Dollar Vibes

The foster care system is an essential part of our society that supports children who are unable to live with their families. However, as these children grow up and reach the age of 18, they are often left without the necessary support and resources to succeed in life. According to the National Foster Youth Institute, over 20,000 young adults age out of the foster care system every year, and only 50% of them will have a job by the age of 24. Additionally, less than 3% of former foster youth earn a college degree. These statistics are alarming and require immediate action.

As a society, we must take care of these young adults and give them the resources they need to succeed. By investing in their education, mental health, and employment opportunities, we can provide them with the tools they need to thrive. And this is where the billion-dollar vibes come in.

The concept of billion-dollar vibes is about creating a positive atmosphere that encourages success and prosperity. It's about creating an environment that fosters growth, empowerment, and inspiration. And this is precisely what we need to provide to foster youth as they transition into adulthood.

By investing in foster youth, we are not only helping them, but we are also helping our society. When we support these young adults, we are giving them the opportunity to become productive members of society. They will be able to contribute to their communities, pay taxes, and positively impact our economy. Therefore, investing in foster youth is not only the right thing to do morally, but it's also the smart thing to do economically.

So, how can we give foster youth billion-dollar vibes? First, we need to provide them with the necessary resources to succeed. This includes access to education, mental health services, and employment opportunities. We need to ensure that every foster youth has access to a quality education, whether that's through vocational training, community college, or a four-year university. We also need to provide them with mental health services to support their emotional well-being and help them overcome any trauma they may have experienced.

Secondly, we need to provide them with employment opportunities. We can do this by partnering with local businesses to provide internships, job training programs, and job placement services. Additionally, we can encourage businesses to provide job opportunities specifically for former foster youth.

Finally, we need to create a sense of community and belonging for foster youth. We can do this by creating mentorship programs that match foster youth with adults who can provide guidance and support. We can also create social events and activities that foster youth to participate in to connect with others who have similar experiences.

In conclusion, giving foster youth aging out of the foster care system billion-dollar vibes is not only the right thing to do, but it's also the smart thing to do. By investing in their education, mental health, and employment opportunities, we can provide them with the necessary resources to succeed. We can create a positive environment that fosters growth, empowerment, and inspiration. And in doing so, we can create a brighter future for fostering youth and our society as a whole.

***

To contact Cheryl:

Please donate and sign up to mentor at fundfc.org or

email cheryl@fundfc.org with any questions about partnerships.

Lindsaya VanDeusen

Lindsaya's journey is one of profound self-discovery and empowerment. Starting as a licensed beauty professional driven by her own desire for personal beauty, she found her true calling in helping others embrace their unique beauty. As the leader of a US territory for an international beauty brand, she combines her expertise with her passion for holistic well-being, guiding individuals towards their wellness goals.

With a deep commitment to self-love and balance, Lindsaya ventured into chakra healing and became a Reiki II practitioner, offering invaluable guidance and support to those seeking alignment. Additionally, she advocates for soil health, recognizing its crucial role in overall well-being and sustainability.

As an event host, Lindsaya brings together diverse individuals, creating transformative experiences that inspire personal growth and self-discovery. In her chapter, "Daily Self-Love Circle," featured in The Change series, she shares insights and practices that amplify the inner Wellness Warrior in each person. This enlightening exploration invites readers to embrace their unique beauty, cultivate self-acceptance, and embark on a joyful and purposeful journey towards holistic well-being.

Lindsaya's wisdom and experiences will leave readers inspired and empowered to embrace self-love and self-empowerment in their lives, fostering a lifelong practice of wellness.

Daily Self-Love Circle
A Transformation Rooted in Self-Love

Lindsaya VanDeusen

Imagine standing in front of a mirror, peering into the depths of your reflection in your birthday suit. Yes, completely naked. Imagine that you begin speaking nicely to yourself instead of focusing on flaws and imperfections. What if you turned the mirror into a window, a gateway into self-discovery and acceptance? That's exactly what I did and continue to do. Then, I began sharing it with the world and inviting others to practice alongside me. Welcome to the Daily Self-Love Circle, where we transform perception into reality, celebrate our uniqueness, honor our journey, and proudly proclaim our truths regarding the light that lives within each of us.

At the tender age of seven, on the playground during second grade, I remember feeling disdain and resentment for my body, sentiments far too complex for a child to grapple with. A psychiatrist later linked these early insecurities to body dysmorphia, an illuminating and disheartening diagnosis -- label.

Born to a single mother grappling with the unthinkable - the recent loss of her sisters and her sister's fiance in a horrific car accident, bookended with the death of her grandparents, followed by her own mother's battle with breast cancer - I found myself arriving and then nestled in a family crippled by unresolved grief and trauma. Shortly after that, my mother entered a marriage with a man who exploited her vulnerability, initiating a cycle of physical and emotional abuse that cast long shadows over my childhood. Later, I bore the brunt of sexual trauma, a painful ordeal that one too many of us have endured.

Whether my narrative echoes your experiences or diverges significantly, I am confident that if you are reading these words, you, too, have known pain and wrestled with your demons. Of course, my story may not mirror yours, but it doesn't have to. We each have experiences that bring us to our knees, and the imprints they leave are as unique as our journeys. It has been my experience, and what so many of the over 75,000 that have participated or attended our circle echo, that these moments contribute to our feelings of unworthiness, shame, resentment, fear, lack of trust, and so much more. And all of these emotions separate us from our brightest light. The vibration of these emotions lowers our vibration and contributes to continuing the cycle. Yet, we are conditioned to believe that if we "sing our praises" or celebrate our success that we are "cocky," "conceited," "boastful," "self-centered," or "egotistical." The irony that we are "supposed to know" our worth but never allow it to leave our lips and are taught never to speak this way about ourselves in front of others is comical when we think about it. When I was growing up, scarcity became a familiar companion, manifesting in a lack of resources, a narrow mindset, and a deficit of emotional nourishment was all I believed I was worth or deserved. Battling body dysmorphia, acne, and obesity, I was locked in a seemingly endless struggle to find comfort in my skin and recognize myself in the mirror without recoiling at the reflection. In my pursuit of worthiness, I spiraled down a path of eating disorders and plastic surgery, my body becoming the canvas of my inner turmoil. A pawn I attempted to update and improve out of a desire to be seen, loved, and desired. I realized I had over-compensated from a place of unworthiness my entire life and that it was showing up in every arena of my life. Learning to say nice things about myself in the mirror in the absence of others was a big step in my development of self-love and confidence. As a Chakra Healer, I first incorporated a 528Hz tuning fork, which led to integrating Solfeggio tones into my mirror work, then with clients at our events and retreats, which led to me becoming a Sound Healer because of the healing I experienced.

In a beautiful twist of fate, I was invited to join the first of what would subsequently be three rounds of Brené Brown's leadership training. I had already consumed everything Brené had shared in the world, and I was so excited to apply it to my own life at a deeper level. During the first round, I was hand selected to join a powerful mastermind of the most beautiful woman from all across the United States, and we created a community of strong, compassionate, heart-led leaders. Then, one of my fellow trainees invited us into a different sacred ritual that would become a keystone of my transformation. Every day, we connected on the app Voxer, sharing three proud moments, three instances of gratitude, and three desires, threading our voices together in a tapestry of empowerment and resilience. This ritual was our daily beacon, lighting our paths for three enriching years. This practice expanded how I saw my life and allowed others to see my dreams alongside me. Yet, one crucial part was still missing, and I became keenly aware of it. All of this optimism, all of the love and gratitude, it was still pouring outwardly. And when I paused and strived to explain why I was proud, grateful, desired, or loved myself the words weren't as easy to find—the awareness regarding how difficult it was when I turned the practice inward was staring me square in the face. I knew this was my doorway deeper.

As I integrated this ritual and discovery of the power of Self-love into mirror work, I recognized the power and expansion that happens when done when speaking and seeing yourself. I came to honor the master manifestor that I am and began permitting myself to lean into my light. Everything in life began to feel more in flow than forced. I host a yearly VisionBoard + Word of the Year Event, and when the word "surrender" came through, I fully embraced it. Things were manifesting quicker than I could keep track of... a trip to Bora Bora, our new home, our children's school, and so many more I could fill this chapter with those wins alone. Then, the event changed the world as we all knew it - Covid-19 and in this isolation, I became more aware and appreciative than ever regarding the importance of community. When the audio app Clubhouse emerged as a new platform for connection, I was curious but not convinced. Social media forums have often felt more like a one-way conversation than social. I didn't believe Clubhouse being social/audio was going to be any different. But all of a sudden, I was connecting with the voices and the hearts of humans from every corner of the globe regarding topics that interest or benefit me and our community. I was making connections and becoming friends with people I would never have imagined nor dreamt of having in my life. It created access to levels of success I couldn't have afforded to get in the room with at that point, as my contract was reduced by half during Covid. At the same time, we had two mortgages because we just closed on our new home and had renovations to be completed to move in and sell our other house. It was an interesting time, and I became much more skilled in DIY than I ever imagined. The silver lining to Clubhouse was that I could be up on a ladder painting, and we could launch our Daily Self-Love Circle or a Wellness Warrior topic, or I could jump into another room and share my knowledge and learn for free.

Inspired by my daily ritual and driven to broaden its reach, I initiated a space in Clubhouse dedicated to self-love on March 6, 2021. Here, I intended to provide a virtual circle where we could practice thinking, believing, and speaking these things about ourselves. It's far more common to speak this way about others. However, in our Daily Self-Love Circle, we permit ourselves to leave everything and everyone else at the door, enter the stage, and unmic to allow our throat chakras to express these ideas and beliefs about Self. We strengthen and create new neural pathways of self-perception, affirming our pride in ourselves, expressing gratitude for pieces of us, visualizing desires as if they are already true, and acknowledging our self-love. Our daily practice that is 2 minutes of less is a testament to our strength, resilience, and limitless potential. And the world is invited.

The ripple effect of this practice created waves of transformation. Nearly 100,000 people have entered the practice. So many have returned and shared the power of their proclamation as they have manifested what they said in the room. We have witnessed businesses launched, evolving careers, new pregnancies, sobriety celebrations, new cars, coveted jobs, and healing in ways beyond our comprehension. We have come to know the power of being witnessed when embodying our truth and how it is amplified when witnessed by others.

The journey of healing and learning to love Self may not be smooth. Recently, I underwent breast explant surgery and facing many challenges. This self-love practice is a lifeline to my Self-love. It is a constant reminder of the inner peace that can be accessed through love. It begins within and for Self. This practice has transcended my vision, blossomed into an incredible community we call Flock, and has been a catalyst for so much healing. In retrospect, I marvel at how this journey unfolded, its humble beginnings, and the expansive growth. Through this Daily Self-Love Circle, I am continually reminded of my capacity to love others, which is directly proportionate to my ability to love myself. I have been so humbled and ignited by the power and way I am positively influenced by what others see and celebrate in Self. Through our practice, I have come to understand that if I desire to embody peace and love, I get to practice finding and expanding my love and acceptance for myself. There is power in bearing witness to our truth and that of others. Doing it in the circle is a remarkable tool for transformation. The journey to self-love is profound, and the destination is a haven of inner peace, strength, and limitless potential. This practice has taught me that one cannot pour from an empty cup. True love, peace, and contentment begin within.

I invite you to come join in the practice. You could scan the QR code and locate where you can find us to practice alongside us live. Or maybe you take the practice to your journal pages first, then the mirror. You may have a laundry list of ways you are proud of yourself, grateful for who you are, a desire you will speak as true, and something you love about yourself. Or, like so many we have met, those ideas feel foreign and distant. Our invitation is to carry this practice with you everywhere you go. Begin to collect evidence that each one is true in abundance. We invite you to use it as your ice breaker in a crowd, a conversation starter at the dinner table, a way to check in with a friend, or encourage someone that doesn't fully see themselves. Share it with your kids, grandkids, colleagues, teams. Our Flock invites you to carry the torch of the P|G|D|L (Proud • Grateful • Desire • Love) into all the communities and relationships you hold most dear.

At the end of our circle, we close our circle with a Lighthouse and invite you to do the same. Every day we complete the shares by proclaiming a Daily Lighthouse. A Lighthouse is a potent reminder of the inherent light within us. It is the beacon of light that guides us back home to ourselves if triggered. In circle everyone declares a word, phrase, verse, or quote- anything anchoring us back to our center and alignment. In honoring our alignment, we live and move in love and abundance.

So where are you going to carry your --

Proud

Grateful

Desire

Love

Once you have made the top of your list, carry these same prompts on to celebrating and honoring those you know, love, or have just met. When we fill our cups first, we can overflow onto the ones we touch and places we show up. Together we will light up the world with the light within us.

***

To contact Lindsaya

Lindsaya VanDeusen

DailySelfLoveCircle.com

Lindsaya.com

Ira S Wolfe

Ira S Wolfe is a Millennial in a Baby Boomer body. Dentist turned futurist, TEDX speaker, 6X author and now Top 5 Global Thought Leader on the future of work, HR and adaptability. There's no one better equipped to help guide you through these Never Normal times with his combination of wisdom, wit, and experience.

Captivated by the exponential speed of change and the volatile, uncertain, complex, and ambiguous world we live in, Ira is thrilled by the possibilities that emerge from novel ideas, human ingenuity, and cutting-edge technology. Yet, the ever-increasing velocity of technological progress also fills him with dread, especially when considering the growing knowledge divide, shifting power dynamics, and widespread naivete.

He is the president and Chief Googlization Officer of Poised for the Future Company, senior consultant with Dame Leadership, and co-host of the top-rated Geeks Geezers Googlization Show podcast. Ira is a TEDx Speaker and 2022 inductee into the HRSouthwest Conference Speaker Hall of Fame. He's co-author of Create Great Culture in a Remote World, and author of Recruiting in the Age of Googlization, consistently nominated to best recruiting and HR book lists. He is a frequent contributor to Forbes and Medium and has been featured in Wall Street Journal, INC Magazine, Fast Company, and dozens more.

From Blahsville to Brilliance, Unleash Your Extraordinary

Ira S. Wolfe

On December 29, 1995, I abandoned my childhood goal. I was 44 years old. On that day, I started living my life.

My story is not unique. The only difference is I took action. You can do the same.

Until that momentous day, it looked like I had it all. I owned a thriving dental practice and was a highly respected, prominent community member in idyllic Amish country, located smack dab between Blue Ball and Intercourse! (I'm not kidding. These are real places. Look them up!) I was married, owned two houses, and had two children and two pets. I was living the American Dream.

What more can one ask for? I was alive and prosperous.

Unfortunately, like countless others, I found myself consumed with a hectic life instead of living it.

And when I say countless, I'm not exaggerating. According to a recent Gallup study, nearly six of every ten workers are not engaged and not thriving. How sad is that? Worse, that's just the tip of the iceberg. One-fifth of people say they are miserable and/or angry. Sixty percent are emotionally detached at work, and 72 percent report feeling lonely at least once a month. Had I been asked to complete this survey nearly 30 years ago, I could have checked off every box - not engaged, not thriving, feeling miserable, sometimes angry, and occasionally lonely.

Oh, and I wasn't just any worker. I was the owner and boss, so I had no one to blame but myself.

Before we go further, let me take you on a quick trip back in time. The place is my 5th-grade class in a small coal mining town in Pennsylvania. The time is the early 1960s.

I remember a defining moment when my teacher, Miss Sedor, asked my class a question that still plays in my head: "What do you want to be when you grow up?" I can even remember the exact location of the desk where I was sitting.

Because Miss Sedor queried my classmates alphabetically, I got to hear the career aspirations of about 25 classmates before she called out, "Wolfe, stand up and tell the class what you want to be."

"A dentist," I announced.

"Good choice," Miss Sedor replied. "You'll make a good dentist. You're smart. You can sit down."

And so it was written in the book of my life. I was going to become a dentist. Book closed.

At the ripe young age of 10, it seemed like I had my entire life mapped out. Whenever one of my parents' friends or even a complete stranger asked me, "What do you want to be when you grow up?," I had a ready-made answer.

Looking back, it's crazy how 10 seconds in 5th grade set me on a course that steered my entire life. I poured my blood, sweat, and tears into every assignment, putting in countless hours of study and sacrifice. It dictated which classes I took and which I dodged like a bullet. It determined which colleges I might attend and opened the doors to the most prestigious dental schools. It probably even influenced which people I met and the friends I made.

And you know what? All that hard work paid off big time, as I crushed every level of education and ranked near the top of every class.

Fast forward to July 1, 1980, nearly two decades after I'd first shared my dream of becoming a dentist with Miss Sedor. Equipped with a staggering $100,000 loan (which was quite the mountain of debt in those days) and a spirit brimming with aspiration, I was all set to conquer the world and make my dreams come true! And boy, did I succeed! From the very first day, my schedule was filled with patients eager to receive my expert care. But, as the clock ticked on and I immersed myself in my career and financial success, I started to experience a disquieting epiphany: my life journey was headed straight to Blahsville and Unfullfiledburg.

For a good fifteen years, my private dental practice was the talk of the town, becoming one of the biggest in the region. I was all in, determined to grow my business, and never shied away from opportunities to innovate and improve. I thought I had found my true calling - my passion. In hindsight, my life was all just smoke and mirrors. A desperate attempt to distract myself from the aimless existence I was living. The buzz of immediate success, the praise and attention, and the thrill of staying busy distracted me from that gnawing feeling that something was missing from my life. As soon as the noise and busyness died, the blah-blah-blahs blared loudly.

I decided to hire an associate, reduce my working hours, golf a few more rounds a week, and purchase a second home on a golf course by the beach. It would seem to most people that my lifestyle and cutting my hours to 20 each week would be a dream come true. But instead of thriving, I was on the brink of burnout. Even the relaxing weekends at my vacation home or on the golf course couldn't erase the stress that came with the thought of returning to the office to drill, fill, and bill.

Don't get me wrong; I had plenty to be grateful for - loyal staff, satisfied patients, and even those heartwarming moments when a dental-phobic patient hugs you and says, "Hey, that wasn't too bad, Doc!" But those moments of fleeting gratification were like a Band-Aid on a gaping wound. While my wallet was flush with cash, my passion and spirit were empty. It wasn't until I was preparing for my 2016 TEDx talk that I finally grasped the truth and uttered these words: "I loved everything about dentistry except the dentistry."

As destiny would have it, the label "dentist" need not confine me. I came to understand that it wasn't the "What" of the actions that fueled and energized me but rather the "Why" and the "How." Like so many others, I had the formula for living a significant and meaningful life all wrong. The journey of that life must be navigated via the GPS of WHY. Regardless of your chosen job or career path, its enchanting appeal may gradually dim if it doesn't pass through WHY.

It took me many years of search and intense self-reflection to finally figure it all out. And during that time, I uncovered something remarkable - my innate ability, a superpower within me all along -

my WHY. And I'm not alone - every single person on this planet has this same superpower. But, sadly, too few of us ever learn how to unleash it.

Even fewer can put it into words. It took me 40 years of trial and error to articulate my WHY, and even now, it's a work in progress.

In the grand scheme of things, it didn't matter whether I was a dentist, teacher, entrepreneur, consultant, blogger, or podcaster. The real significance stemmed not from my job title or my work but from the authentic purpose that energized me and the meaningful, lasting effect it created.

Let me level with you—I won't pretend I've stumbled upon some mystical secret. Sure, I've navigated life's often weird path and unexpected detours and have experienced the rewards and scars to prove it. But along the way, I've discovered that genuine happiness and satisfaction don't stem from what I did and the things I accumulated. Instead, they're rooted in something far more profound and beautifully simple.

That's what prompted me, 28 years ago, to take a daring plunge, bid farewell to my practice, and truly start living. Reflecting on that choice, I can confidently say it was the best decision of my life. My only regret is that I had not made the decision earlier.

Today my goal, or should I say my purpose, is to help others live an extraordinary and meaningful life, and hope to do it in much less time than it took me.

Together, let's unlock your superpower - your WHY - and start living a life of purpose and fulfillment beyond your wildest dreams. Let's get started!

Break Free from Your Familiarity Machine

I think we can all agree - the future at this point seems like one big crapshoot. That's a problem because humans have been programmed to seek stability and safety. In fact, neuroscience research suggests that humans may be addicted to certainty and that our brains have become familiarity machines. So how does one make the changes required to live a meaningful and purpose-filled life when we are bombarded with the allure of job titles and measured by the glitz of material accumulation?

I'll be the first to admit that living your WHY and purpose is not a cakewalk. Living your WHY is a journey full of ups and downs, twists and turns. With the world in constant flux, it feels as if we've been blindfolded and spun around, trying to pin the tail on a constantly moving donkey. We're never quite certain where we'll land. Life's disorienting nature means we're bound to stumble and make errors along the way.

But here's the thing - the most successful and resilient people know these bumps and detours are just part of the ride. They know mistakes are not failures but merely opportunities to learn and grow. The key to success, then, is to learn to make change work for you. And that begins with a growth mindset.

Now, I wish I could take credit for this discovery. I can't. Full credit goes to the brilliant Dr. Carol Dweck. She's a professor at Stanford University who, over thirty years ago, introduced the world to two essential concepts: the fixed mindset and the growth mindset. And let me tell you, her findings are more relevant now than ever before in today's Never Normal world. Personally, I can't even imagine making the life changes I've made without adopting a growth mindset. It's amazing what a shift in perspective can do!

So, what is a fixed and growth mindset?

Dweck discovered these are two different ways we think about our abilities and potential. People with a fixed mindset are more likely to give up, back down, and avoid challenges than those with a growth mindset. For example, have you ever heard anyone say, "I'm not good at math." Or maybe it's not being good at public speaking, playing sports, or managing people. A fixed mindset is when we believe that we're either good or bad at something and there's nothing we can do to change it. The fixed mindset motto is "We are who we are." A growth mindset, on the other hand, manifests when we believe we can develop and improve our abilities through hard work, practice, and not giving up. The world becomes one big Yeti Challenge: "I'm just not good at math … yet-I … will find a tutor and practice."

If you have a fixed mindset, you might get really anxious or even depressed when things don't go your way. You'll do almost anything to avoid the embarrassment of making a mistake or failing.

Is it any wonder that people stay in jobs, careers, and even relationships long past their due date? The fixed mindset voices in our heads focus on "what happens if I submit my application and don't hear back? What if I don't interview well? What if I really want the new job and get rejected?"

Alternatively, if you have a growth mindset, you view change and challenges as opportunities for learning and growth. Sports legend and hockey great Wayne Gretsky once said, "You miss 100% of the shots you don't take." That epitomizes a growth mindset. We believe that even if we fail at something, we can learn from it and improve next time.

Others often suggest that it took a lot of guts, courage, and boldness for me to walk away from my thriving practice and start a new career. Here's the thing. I never felt it was brave, courageous, or bold. It felt completely natural. I was relieved! The change I made on that momentous day resulted from silencing the distracting, cacophonous fixed mindset voices in my head and allowing my growth mindset to narrate my life journey.

With my bags packed and an abundant supply of energy and enthusiasm, I was ready for my next adventure. But without a clear, articulated purpose, I fell into the same trap I thought I had left behind. My life felt like a Sunday joy ride - a lot of fun with no destination.

That is until I could find and articulate my WHY.

Find Your WHY

Articulating our WHY in a way that unleashes the extraordinary life within you is much easier said than done. You would think that being a keynote speaker and the author of over a thousand articles and six books, I could easily compose a straightforward sentence explaining my WHY. But no matter what combination of words I strung together or how hard I tried, It was like pulling teeth! How crazy is that? Words that should just roll off my tongue as quickly and autonomously as the air I breathe in and out; I choked on them repeatedly.

Putting your purpose into words can be challenging - it's like trying to describe a color that doesn't exist or describing the taste of your favorite food in a language you don't speak. It's a bit like trying to explain to your grandma how to use an iPhone! You know what you want to say, but finding the right words can be a real challenge. Of course, it doesn't help that your purpose may be tied to a specific set of experiences or passions that are hard to define.

Despite all these challenges, it's essential and well worth it to keep working towards putting your purpose into words. The more you reflect on your values, passions, and experiences, the clearer your purpose will become. And once you can put your purpose into words, you'll feel like a superhero with a clear mission to save the world.

It wasn't until I came across something called the Golden Circle and a tool based on our 9 WHYs that I was able to unleash my superpower and shift my focus from what I do to WHY.

Before I reveal those 9 WHYs, let me provide some background and context because you might wonder what WHY has to do with what we do or how we do what we do. (Yikes! That's a lot of what!)

From What to WHY

The Golden Circle is a concept developed by leadership thought leader Simon Sinek that helps us understand what makes successful companies and individuals stand out from the rest. It's a bullseye with three circles.

The center "why" circle represents a clear sense of purpose or belief that guides everything you do. The middle "how" circle represents your unique approach or process to achieve your goals. And the outer "what" circle reveals the impact you want to have through the products or services you offer.

The mistake most people make is they start with what and work from the outside in. What sets successful companies and individuals apart is that they start on the inside: with why not what.

Unleashing the Extraordinary You

Are you now ready to uncover your unique WHY? The reason that drives you to make an impact and live life to its fullest potential? Let's explore the nine WHYs and discover what makes you extraordinary.

CONTRIBUTE: To Contribute to a Greater Cause, Make a Difference, Add Value, or Have an Impact

You're a team player who lives to impact the world if your WHY is to Contribute. You thrive on adding value, supporting others, and being part of something bigger than yourself. Nothing brings you more joy than seeing the team succeed.

Do you believe you have the WHY to Contribute?

TRUST: To Create Relationships Based on Trust

Trust is your bread and butter. Trust is the secret sauce to any relationship; you're all about making sure people know they can count on you. In addition, you're constantly honing your skills and knowledge to be the go-to person in your area of expertise.

Do you believe you have the WHY to Trust?

MAKE SENSE: To Make Sense Out of Things

You possess a remarkable passion for finding simplicity in complexity if your WHY is to Make Sense. You use your unique gift to bring order to chaos and make sense of it all.

Do you believe you have the WHY to Make Sense?

BETTER WAY: To Find a Better Way and Share it

As a Better Way thinker, you're the ultimate innovator! You're always looking for ways to improve even the most minor things. Your passion and drive to improve everything are contagious and motivate others to aim for greater heights.

Do you believe you have the WHY to Better way?

RIGHT WAY: To Do Things the Right Way

If your WHY is the Right Way, you're a stickler for following the right procedures and systems to achieve success. Doing things the right way helps you achieve your goals and make a positive impact.

Do you believe you have the WHY to do things the Right way?

CHALLENGE: To Think Different and Challenge the Status Quo

If you live by the Challenge WHY you're no follower. You're not content playing life safe. Instead, you relish pushing boundaries and defying convention. You see rules as mere suggestions and believe life may be more exciting outside the proverbial box.

MASTERY: To Seek Mastery

If your WHY is Mastery, you're like a sponge, absorbing all the knowledge you can get your hands on! You find pure joy in the journey of learning and enjoy sharing your knowledge with others.

Do you believe you have the WHY of Mastery?

CLARITY: To Create Clarity

If your WHY is Clarity, you won't stop until your message is crystal clear. You believe being understood is vital. Language is your playground, and you love using creative analogies and metaphors to communicate your point.

Do you believe you have the WHY of Clarity?

SIMPLIFY: To Simplify

Making life easier for everyone around you is your passion if your WHY is to Simplify. You're passionate about finding ways to streamline processes and cut unnecessary steps, no matter how complicated the situation is.

Do you believe you have the WHY of Simplify?

Your WHY is Almost Within Reach

So what is my WHY, you may ask?

It is to help others find a better way to be extraordinary, grow and thrive outside their comfort zones, and never settle for anything less than what they're capable of achieving.

Are you now ready to Unlock YOUR WHY like I did? You can learn more at https://UnlockMyWhy.com.

Now it's time to put YOUR WHY, How, and What to work so that it sparks your calling and inspires others to want to support and join you on your journey.

Whether you want to make a difference, create connections, pursue knowledge, achieve excellence, lead, innovate, serve, enjoy life, or challenge the status quo, there's nothing you can't achieve and experience with a growth mindset and your WHY.

Ready, set, go!

***

To contact Ira:

     Website: irawolfe.com
     Website: adaptabilitytoolkit.com or adaptability.expert
     Podcast: Geeks Geezer Googlization
     Community: googlizationnation.com
     Newsletter: NeverNormalNews
     Forbes:
     forbes.com/sites/forbescoachescouncil/people/irawolfe/
     Email: ira+growthmindset@irawolfe.com
     LinkedIn: linkedin.com/in/irawolfe
     YouTube: youtube.com/irawolfe
     Twitter: @hireauthority

Check out Ira's previous books:
     Recruiting in the Age of Googlization (2nd edition)
     Create Great Culture in a Remote World
     Geeks, Geezers, and Googlization
     Understanding Business Values and Motivators
     Perfect Labor Storm 2.0
     Perfect Labor Storm Fact Book

Nancey Sinclaire

Nansey was adopted in Argentina as a newborn baby. Her family travelled and lived in various parts of the world before moving to Canada and calling it home.

A mother of three – one boy and two girls - life challenged Nansey with the two girls being physically disabled, requiring daily special attention and care.

Her own difficult background and the upbringing of her children exposed one of her many extraordinary talents: she became a lifelong learner with an insatiable quest for knowledge and an unquenchable curiosity about life. This helped her tremendously with seeking and finding the right and most effective care for her two daughters, mentally, emotionally, and physically.

Nansey believes her positive mindset and her determination, together with her commitment and dedication to her children have shaped and influenced her personal growth in profound ways.

A passionate and an enthusiastic person she believes the Universe is always conspiring for our good.

Her desire is to raise the level of compassion and kindness in the world starting with ourselves.

A writer she has co-authored The Mystery of a Woman 2011, 1000 Tips for Teenagers 2012, The Change Volume 4 2015, The Change Volume 19 2023 and is currently writing her first children's book due to be published 2023.

She's a certified diver, an industrious businesswoman, pet lover, amateur photographer and currently lives on Vancouver Island, B.C. Canada.

Determined To Defeat My Daughters Diabetes Diagnosis

By Nancey Sinclaire

As with most of us, I've had my share of ups and downs, challenges, difficulties, and obstacles to overcome in life.

Some of my challenges include being divorced twice, raising three children as a single parent, the birth and delivery of my firstborn by emergency C-section, bankruptcy, being adopted in a foreign country and disowned as an adult by my adoptive parents, parent alienation from two of my children, and recovery from PTSD.

My daughters, mirror identical image twins, born three and a half months premature, suffered significant brain bleeds, resulting in a diagnosis of Spastic Diplegic Cerebral Palsy. As a result, they have no core strength, cannot stand or sit, and depend on wheelchairs for their mobility.

Complications throughout the pregnancy, during birth, and after delivery were undoubtedly some of my life's scariest experiences.

Twenty-seven years later, all those experiences seem to pale compared to the fear and trepidation I felt when our family doctor delivered the news in December of 2019 that one of my daughters had been diagnosed with type two diabetes. I knew nothing about diabetes, either type one or type two.

The doctor wrote a prescription and told me it was an irreversible diagnosis she'd have for the rest of her life that could only be managed with medication.

She briefly explained some of the significant concerns and ramifications associated with diabetes, then contacted the diabetes resource team at the hospital and arranged for them to reach out to me.

My daughter began Metformin the next day—the standard medication prescribed by doctors for newly diagnosed patients.

I began studying the effects and symptoms of type two diabetes and anxiously waited for a call from the clinic to arrange our three-hour training and orientation session. We came home with a 67-page educational document about diabetes. My mind was overloaded; my head was spinning. I was emotionally exhausted and completely overwhelmed. I felt nervous, scared, and panicked about how, where, and when to start to take the steps necessary to turn this situation around.

I knew nothing about diabetes. I was shocked to learn how detrimental diabetes can be to a person's health. It was vital to control my daughter's sugar levels immediately. Her liver, kidneys, heart, and feet could be adversely affected if it wasn't managed quickly and regulated through prescription medication.

I learned that diabetes increases the chances of long-term complications such as heart attack, stroke, amputation, and blindness. Also, there is the risk of high blood pressure, high blood sugar, and abnormal blood fats, which can cause damage to blood vessels and nerves. I've since learned of an individual who has lost their eyesight and had their foot amputated because of diabetes.

I was horrified to learn if a person becomes hypoglycemic, they could go into a coma.

My daughter is 37 years old. The complications from birth resulted in other complexities over and above her cerebral palsy.

She has epilepsy, a significant cognitive delay. She is incontinent, has sleep apnea, and uses a CPAP machine nightly to keep her airways open while sleeping.

She depends on others twenty-four-seven for all her personal and physical care needs and has no intellectual understanding of what diabetes is.

I wondered how much more complicated it would become to care for her immobile body and cognitively delayed mind. Would I be able to tell if she was dehydrated and if her sugar levels were too high or too low? What if I missed something? What If something happened to her and she had to go to the hospital? What if she had to go to the hospital in an ambulance and I wasn't there to explain to the attendants her diagnosis of cerebral palsy and how it affects her? She wouldn't be able to communicate with them adequately. They could administer a treatment that could adversely affect her health without prior knowledge of her disability.

How was I possibly going to retain all this information?

The booklet described symptoms indicating when it was time to seek urgent medical care. Symptoms include blurred vision, stomach pain, weakness, confusion, and urinating, either more or less than usual.

It also described how symptoms of depression, such as feeling sad, having little or no energy, changes in sleep patterns, changes in appetite, and trouble concentrating can make it more difficult to manage diabetes.

How would I be able to distinguish the difference between those symptoms being caused by her diabetes or by her epilepsy and cognitive delays since she experiences many of those symptoms regularly? I felt the pressure mounting.

The level of my responsibility for the care and nurture of another human being increased tenfold. I was scared to leave her side. How could I possibly explain all these details to the caregivers who tend to her needs when I'm not at the house and trust that they wouldn't miss anything in her behavior that would indicate she needed urgent medical care?

How would I possibly know if she had blurred vision since she's unable to indicate if she's having issues with her eyesight?

My learning curve was steep. I would have to track her sugar glucose levels throughout the day to determine if her sugars were too high and/or too low and then figure out what to do.

I was utterly intimidated and confused about figuring out the sugar levels.

If her blood sugars were over 14.0 mmol/l before meals or bedtime on two tests in a row **AND** her urine ketones were moderate or large, 1.5 mmol/l or higher, it was time to take her to the emergency room at the hospital.

As a student, I had always struggled with math, and here it was to haunt me. I had no idea what mmol/L meant. I felt intimidated, scared, and stupid. What if I couldn't figure it out? What would happen to my daughter? Would I ultimately be responsible for not caring for her and ensuring her optimum health?

Twelve days after she started the metformin, the gynecologist's office called as I was leaving my Pilates class with an urgent message that her blood work results had come back. Her iron levels were deficient, and she needed to get to the hospital **immediately** for a blood transfusion.

"Thank God," I noticed the phone ringing as I climbed into my vehicle to head home from class. What if I missed the call? What if I hadn't spoken to the doctor? What if I'd gone straight home and gone to bed? She could have bled out during the night, and it would have been my fault. What a nightmare! "What if" thoughts ran through my head, a chill running down my spine. I called ahead to the caregiver.

I instructed her to get my daughter dressed and out of bed into her wheelchair with her coat on. I told her to pack the items my daughter would need to take to the hospital: her medical card, a sling for all transfers in and out of her wheelchair, clothing, medication, briefs, wipes, and liners for her incontinence. There was no way to know how long we'd be there. I had to be prepared.

Time was of the essence; I had to move quickly and calmly to get her there safely. The time involved in loading her in and out of the vehicle, parking, and buying a parking ticket all added to the mounting pressure and stress of getting her attended to as soon as possible.

Six days after her blood transfusion, I rushed her to the hospital emergency for excruciating abdominal pain. She woke up in the morning and suddenly started screaming out in pain. One of the caregivers advised me that she was trying to gain attention and that nothing was wrong.

We arrived at the hospital at 9:00 a.m. She was in agony the entire day as doctors, nurses, and lab techs poked and prodded her to determine a prognosis. Finally, at midnight the surgeon performed emergency exploratory surgery and removed her appendix, which was just about to burst. They'd gotten to it in the nick of time.

They discovered her abdomen was septic with infection. She was bleeding internally; she had a bladder infection. Her lungs were filled with fluid. She had pneumonia. Additionally, the metformin prescribed for her diabetes was causing continuous unstoppable diarrhea.

She was in anguish. The sounds of her cries were ear-piercing, and I could do little to take away the pain. She was helpless, and I felt powerless.

After surgery, she was admitted to the ward critically ill. The doctors continued to assess her condition. The days were filled with X-rays, CT scans, Ultrasounds, and blood tests—examinations from doctors and specialists attempting to determine the next course of action to aid her recovery.

Her heart rate, oxygen levels, blood pressure, and glucose levels were constantly monitored. Although she received pain medication, antibiotics, and fluids intravenously and remained on oxygen, her condition continued to decline.

More time, more anguish, more waiting, more testing, more of the unknown. More of a wait and see.

It was an emotional and mental rollercoaster for days on end. Minute to minute, hour to hour, we didn't know which way was up.

Three and a half weeks later in January 2020, she was discharged from the hospital. Her recovery was long, slow, and complicated. The world was at a standstill; she was utterly exhausted and now susceptible to Covid.

The Diabetes Resource team and the doctor continued prescribing different medications to manage her diabetes.

I spoke at length with the doctor about my desire and intention to get her diabetes managed with natural methods versus pharmaceutical means, even though she was adamant that prescription medication was the only option.

I dove in with both feet, determined to learn everything I needed to understand what was causing the diabetes and what we needed to do differently to reverse the diagnosis and/or get it under control with methods other than prescription drugs.

I researched, purchased, and studied various books, magazines, and articles on and offline. I joined a six-week online plant-based food workshop focused on individuals with diabetes. Every week there was a panel of experts in the field facilitating classes and educating the viewers in all aspects of health related to diabetes. They shared menu planning and explained how to read nutritional labels to count carbs, fibers, and sugars in foods. They helped me determine what she could eat, how much, and how often. I attended the live classes, listened to, and studied the replays repeatedly to ensure I'd absorbed all the information.

I went up and down every aisle in the grocery store, read and compared labels on every container or package on the shelf as I educated myself on how to stay within the parameters of what she could eat to manage her diabetes naturally.

I eliminated meat and dairy from her diet and introduced plant-based food. Increased her daily intake of fresh vegetables, weighed, and measured her food, and created a menu plan for her meals and snacks, totaling her daily allowance for carbs, sugars, and fibers.

We increased the amount of water she drank daily, tracked, and scheduled everything she ate and drank. I introduced bitter melon tea and smoothies made with protein powder and greens.

The physiotherapist created a daily stretching routine for the caregivers to implement to circulate the insulin in her body.

Being overweight and underactive contributes to diabetes, and she's unable to exercise due to her cerebral palsy.

My days were consumed with hours of study, research, planning, and implementation of my findings. It was emotionally, mentally, and physically exhausting.

Her A1C levels were tested every three months.

A1C tests measure the average sugar glucose readings over a three-month period. It's a method to determine if a person falls within the target range of healthy sugar levels of 7 or below. Initially diagnosed with A1C level readings over 13, we had to cut them in half to avoid the threat of taking insulin regularly.

The idea of her taking insulin was terrifying. I was determined it would not become necessary.

The diabetes nurse advised I would have to take a finger prick several times throughout the day to check her glucose levels to determine if they were within the appropriate range.

I didn't have the emotional capacity to prick the end of her finger and squeeze out some blood to test it. When hospitalized, the nurses constantly pricked her finger to check her glucose level. It wrenched my heart as I watched her in so much pain and discomfort.

The year progressed with changes to her diet. Adjusting the metformin and introducing other prescribed medications to help manage the release of insulin into her body. It was a long, arduous process for several months to determine if the adjustments were effective.

Her seizure activity increased and became frightening.

The pharmacist recommended a continuous glucose monitoring system she could use on her arm instead of a finger prick to track her sugar levels. A small round sensor is inserted into her arm that is replaced every two weeks.

I purchased the system in 2022, read the instructions, and prepared to insert the sensor into her arm. My left hand fractured, and arthritis in the same hand; opening the package and inserting the sensor into the mechanism was excruciating, awkward, and challenging.

I sat beside her and held her arm against mine. My body was overcome with fear. I began to shake, tears welled up, and my chest and stomach tightened. I felt nauseated. I feared hurting her. The sight of the needle on the underside of the sensor terrified me. I played calming music, took deep breaths, said a prayer, pressed the mechanism and inserted the sensor. Immediately after, I ran upstairs to the spare bedroom, curled up in a fetal position, and cried my heart out.

I was instantly flooded with memories of her premature birth, her vulnerability, and the suffering she had experienced. I pictured her delicate, fragile, naked, two-pound body in her incubator.

Her head to one side, eyes closed, and tubes taped to her face. Delicate wires attached to her head and body. Her every breath and bodily function were monitored. Alarms beeping to alert the nurses that she needed immediate care. I recalled her translucent skin that exposed the veins in her body when she laid on the warming table in the operating room. Her legs were positioned like the shape of a frog. Her body was black and blue with bruises from her sister kicking her in utero.

Inserting the sensor was the catalyst that triggered a rush of emotional pain buried deep within my subconscious. A reservoir of sadness from when she was born and all the challenges, struggles, and obstacles she faced in her lifetime washed over me.

I was even more determined that she would never have to take insulin shots.

Her blood sugar levels sometimes dropped to a dangerous low reading of 3. She would have to chew 4-5 pure sugar Dex tablets, wait fifteen minutes, take a reading, and repeat if the readings were still low.

It was nerve-wracking every time her sugar levels dropped. The question was always what to do next if it didn't improve. Would this be the time to call the ambulance to have her rushed to the emergency room?

The benefit of the sensor system is that the information can be downloaded to create charts and graphs that reflect how her body functions throughout the day. Peaks and valleys are pinpointed, which aids in deciphering the next course of action—another huge learning curve for me.

I felt a tremendous sense of relief within the first six months as her A1C 3-month average levels were cut in half primarily because of the prescribed medication.

I continued to monitor her food intake, preparing and cooking plant-based meals daily. We eliminated two of the prescribed medications.

And in the spring of 2023, I became very concerned about the pattern of low-level readings that seemingly appeared out of the blue.

Nothing had changed regarding her food intake, although her stress levels had increased. For a few consecutive days, they dipped to below a 3, and she had to take the pure sugar dex tablets and orange juice repeatedly before any improvement in her readings.

I sent the downloaded reports to the diabetes nurse for review, booked an appointment with the doctor, and nervously anticipated and dreaded the only resolution would be to increase her prescription of Metformin.

March 29th, 2023, I was elated when I received a call from the diabetes nurse to congratulate me on my efforts to manage my daughter's diabetes through food. She concluded that the prescribed medication was the cause of her blood sugar levels dipping too low. She confirmed that although there were dips in her blood sugar levels during the latter part of the day, it was evident that the lows were being managed by food. She no longer had to continue with Metformin.

It was all I could do to contain my excitement. I couldn't stop crying. Flooded with joy, tears running down my eyes, I called her dad, teaming with delight as I reveled in announcing that I'd accomplished my goal. Her diabetes was now under control and managed by food, and she was no longer dependent on prescription drugs.

The process took just shortly over two years. It took a lot of dedication, commitment, and belief that it was possible. It was a laborious, stressful, and exhaustive process; however, it was successful.

Two days later, my daughter and I sat in the doctor's office with tears in my eyes. I shared how overjoyed I was with the news that she no longer required the use of prescription medication to manage her diabetes.

I gently reminded her of my initial intentions to achieve this outcome. She looked me in the eye, congratulated me, and said, **"It's rare Nansey, it's rare."**

***

To contact Nansey:

250-268-4493

nanseysinclaire@gmail.com

https://www.facebook.com/nanseysinclaire

https://www.linkedin.com/in/nanseysinclaire/

Darcee D. McJannet

Global Thought Leader, Best Selling Author, Advisor, Work-Life Rebalance Authority, Purpose Driven Humanitarian & Social Impact Entrepreneur, Global Peace & Human Rights Advocate

Darcee D. McJannet CEO & Founder of Stratego Consulting International created a socially conscious company committed to elevating humanity. A visionary thinker and creative genius, her ideas and strategic solutions exemplify her high-level advisory expertise. Darcee is dynamic, direct, multi-talented and tenacious with a fierce work ethic and strong determination to see others succeed. Her refreshing and innovative approach imparts wisdom to assist others with their life purpose and becoming the best version of themselves. A smart, savvy stabilizer who consolidates chaos. Her methodology encompasses leadership development, executive and life coaching, work-life rebalance and wellness integration. An empath with heightened intuition and an analytical approach equal profound insights to accelerate transformation and a rebalanced mind, body, and soul.

Mentored by the World's Best experts. Media trained from Oprah's producer in New York. A true "Leadership Diva," with style and substance. Co-featured in "The Game Changer" movie. Her diverse business background harnesses 30 years of experience in 24 business sectors. Corporate experience includes successfully leading cross-functional teams as a regional executive manager at IBM. Guest speaker at academic institutions. Attained a double major degree in Business Administration & Political Science, thesis dissertation for MBA on Corporate Wellness. Certified International Coach, with numerous accreditations.

Effective Living to Rebalance

By: Darcee D. McJannet

With over eight billion people on the planet, large segments of the population are struggling to navigate the complexities and changing dynamics of a globalized economy that burdens individuals to find ways to manage the demanding, and often unforgiving shifting realities. Although, technological advancement and innovation are a double-edge sword, offering both efficiencies, along with societal stressors. The pursuit of happiness, passion projects, and spiritual enrichment is a luxury for many, overshadowed by life's burdens and replaced by negative feelings of energy depletion, depression, stress, anxiety, and an overwhelming sense of chaos. The search for sustainable solutions is driven by the prevalent desire to mitigate the soul-destroying feeling of a life spiraling out of control, where family, friends, health, careers, and personal satisfaction are a consequence of a life not aligned or in balance.

After decades of researching human and organizational behavior in personal and professional development and observing the world's systemic problems, I felt a heavy calling to elevate humanity. Combining my life experiences, academic background, and ability as an empath, I formulated a *"Rebalance"* framework compiling and condensing vital information to successfully manage the integration of one's personal and professional life. Rebalance is a holistic approach that considers the totality of the body, mind, and soul unique to each person. A rebalance strategy for individual wellness unequivocally works and it remarkably restored my health against insurmountable odds to overcome a diagnosis of lupus, cancer, fibromyalgia, and a concussion. I embody these transformational principles and have experienced miraculous healing from a holistic integration and healthy lifestyle. Through the integration of a rebalanced trifecta your mind, body, and soul operate in tandem to feel restored, rejuvenated, and renewed. Successfully rebalancing your life begins with your mindset. Mental resilience is a choice, and we can choose to be victims of circumstance or take control of our lives to create a new reality. Intergenerational thought patterns are important for impartation and leaving a legacy. I was raised to be emotionally strong and embrace the philosophy "that there is *no such thing as can't.*" Your belief system travels with you your entire life like subconscious baggage, so it is imperative to empower your thoughts. The capacity to heal oneself begins in the mind, prior to it manifesting within the body.

It is essential for your overall wellbeing to intentionally reset and refocus. In an era of detrimental distraction, individuals are inundated with devices and cell phone fixations, fast tracking often irrelevant information that consumes their time. Communication inundation through mainstream media, social media, and advertisements target your digital footprint to make a people feel connected, while simultaneously disconnected and lost. The exorbitant use of screen time has desensitized children and adults to sensory stimuli and programmed them for instant gratification. Video gaming addictions have taken over what was once an innocent past time for mindful redirection to infiltrate our youth into being tethered to a virtual world. Escapism offers little appreciation for the rewards of a balanced life, nor does it satisfy the soul in the long-term. It is important to look inward for self-fulfillment because external rewards are fleeting.

The global pandemic unfairly impacted people's lives and livelihoods exasperating stress levels. Thus, triggering global governmental interventions, societal and economic changes, lock downs and travel restrictions. Overburdened healthcare systems, frontline worker exhaustion, vaccine and mask mandate controversy, contentious social interactions with conflicting philosophies. Online education forced parents to become pseudo teachers while simultaneously working, fast paced technological advancement created a deeper digital divide, artificial intelligence concerns continue, deep fakes, digital manipulation, cyber security and hacking impacted infrastructure, ATMs, currency, stocks plummeting, negatively impacting retirement portfolios, digital analytics with online profiling is usurping privacy and personal freedoms and a threat to the fabric of democracy, inflation, soaring costs, negative news cycles resulted in the inability for people to decipher between opinion and fact. Global protests, war, supply chain disruptions, climate change, cyberbullying, cancel culture, online censorship are trying to starve people into submission.

Individuals are still processing pandemic losses from isolation and confusion. The never-ending barrage of daily demands navigating the gauntlet of responsibilities and obligations with family, children, school, health and medical appointments, aging parents, friends, work, volunteering all create immense overwhelm. Let's face it, life is hard!

The solution to a new normal is adopting a hopeful *"optimistic adaptation mindset"* to thrive and not just survive. Emerging innovation and technology with electric vehicles have been great for the environmental impact, however produced a new phenomenon of *charging anxiety* whereby individuals have a mental preoccupation worrying about running out of battery life for electric vehicles, while calculating every micro detail to charging locations. Stress is systemic and prior to the pandemic, 58% of individuals reported feeling "overloaded" and struggled from a work life balance perspective. Global burnout rates skyrocketed with the pandemic and in the United States, 2 in 5 employees indicated feeling overwhelmed and suffered from work-related burnout. This further substantiates the need for a sustainable and productive 4-day work week. This business model is effective for professional occupations; however, it is not possible for all positions or entrepreneurs. A built-in long weekend allows time for short trips and rejuvenation, returning to work rested and highly productive. Europeans have mastered the art of work life rebalance.

Researchers discovered employee attrition changed with people exiting current roles for different positions or leaving the workforce to pursue a better quality of life. Individuals have functioned under extreme conditions for an extended time unable to find their work life balance equilibrium. Those returning to the workplace want flexibility, competitive compensation, and reasonable performance expectations. What is evident is the apparent need to regain control and autonomy over our decisions and lives again. The global pandemic caused individuals to become introspective and question their mortality and happiness. We need to reclaim and restore our lives as we emerge with a resilient mindset. Resist self-imposed mental limitations and artificial societal constructs. You are never defined by your circumstances; only on how proactively and reactively you respond to them.

Success is a unique journey speckled by personal experiences; the important thing is to remain committed to continuous self-improvement. What one person deems successful, another may not. The common denominator of personal and professional achievement is based on foundational thinking and a series of incremental steps forward to navigate unexpected circumstances. The ability to adapt and pivot are core elements to problem solving and achieving success. An expansive mindset with abstract thinking opens more possibilities for fulfilment than a rigid linear sequential approach.

I developed a guide of principles and strategies to assist individuals at any stage or age to manage the chaos of competing priorities, identify unique and inherent coping strategies to enhance productivity and mitigate barriers disrupting a healthy approach to effective life management.

You can begin to *Rebalance* your life by creating *positive daily disruptors* that offset and reduce the amount of environmental negativity as a built-in redirection system.

It is more important to be purposeful and consciously avoid being a victim of indecision or apathy. Going through the motions of life uninspired without direction or purpose results in a person becoming a *"Directionless bystander"* with few expectations and personal successes. Exist in the moment, persevere through obstacles, resist negative thoughts, and hold yourself accountable to a rebalance strategy that enriches your life. Focus on things that support your wellbeing, while limiting energy depleting activities that lead to *"unbalanced dissatisfaction."* Be true to yourself, remain positive, and thrive in your new rebalanced reality. Continuous mental recalibration is necessary to adapt to complex challenges and mitigate stress. Rebalance by mentally adjusting and pivoting quickly to evolve and accept that nothing stays static, nor should it. It is paramount to proactively ride the ebbs and flows of your physical and mental energy, to optimize results during peak periods of focus and recharge when your resolve and commitment is at lower energy levels.

Rebalancing is a holistic and proactive lifestyle philosophy and paradigm that encompasses your personal and professional life, to establish a hierarchy of mandatory objectives, optimal goals, and internal resources (time, energy, health, etc.) Excellence in any field commands and demands dedication, perseverance & endurance to achieve anything. A rebalanced mindset responds with calm clarity, able to reason with less emotional attachment. You function from a deeper purpose and higher frequency, allowing for less resistance and greater flow. A rebalanced lifestyle enables you to be self-actualized, grounded in a sense of contentment, gratitude, and inner peace. Moreover, most people inherently know their trigger points for unhealthy, unproductive, and destructive behavior, however struggle to find effective physical and mental models to cope with increasing stressors.

It is critically important to maintain a consistent healthy baseline for your body, mind, and soul. Personal progress holds no short cuts, it requires time, discipline, and focus. Individuals that excel have refined and efficient time management strategies, recognizing time is not a renewable resource, but a precious finite commodity. Double down on what works, leverage resources at your disposal and commit to the process of continuous self-improvement and heightened self-awareness.

The unfortunate reality is that if you don't evolve and adapt you get left behind in a cloud of regret. The *universal law of adaptation* is a survival of the fittest mentality. An abundance mindset has the willingness to sacrifice and persevere to successfully rebalance.

Reaching your full potential to be the best version of yourself requires an intentional steadfast fearless commitment. Personal progress operates on a long-term foundational mindset and continuous recommitment to keep showing up when it gets difficult. Do the inner work necessary to be your healthiest and happiest self. Mental resilience is controlling our internal responses to everything despite our external circumstances. To prevent getting stuck in a negative emotional vortex when life deals you bad breaks or unfair, unplanned circumstances, you need to emotionally modulate and keep moving forward.

Your resolve and internal commitment to yourself and those that depend on you must be a strong stabilizing anchor to sustain you in challenging times. Life by design is not an accidental coincidence, it requires daily mental flossing. Intentional action harnesses our goals to leave a generational legacy and teach the next generation healthy mindset and lifestyle habits. Mental management is vital to overcome burnout and emotional unwellness.

Rebalance is grounded in the notion that you intentionally create an *optimization zone* to function at your highest ability. Find your equilibrium and peak performance zone to be your best. Optimization techniques translate into being in a state of overflow with increased confidence, opportunities, and internal stamina. A recent study investigated the brain processes underlying the positive effects on stress from walking in nature for an hour to reset. This is an incredible and inexpensive mobile meditation method to reboot your mental state. In Japan *forest bathing* is incorporated into their national health initiative. This conscious contemplative process has been scientifically proven to positively rewire brain patterns. I termed this *Mindful Redirection,* an approach to recalibrate your thought process and clear your brain while redirecting your emotional state. Painting, decorating, gardening, working out, automotive, gaming, photography, passion projects allow you to reboot and reframe your mind to replenish your energy.

Rebalance strategies and tools are designed to effectively tackle unforeseen obstacles, manage life, and allow for greater happiness and a reality that remains in equilibrium. Approaching life *unconsciously, living* with no sense of direction or purpose is a recipe for *unbalanced dissatisfaction,* resulting in hopelessness, anxiety, stress disorders, depression, and overall malaise. To achieve your desired results, devise a conscious strategic life plan and vision to enact it. Once centered in a state of rebalanced alignment your reality takes on a life of its own, filled with passion and purpose. Carefully consider what truly ignites your spirit. A persistent positive approach, focused on time management and goal prioritization are core elements to work-life prioritization. Formulating new patterns and neuropathways involves analyzing your pre-existing paradigms and regular routines. Pair healthy habits together, so that one triggers the activation of the next.

To successfully rebalance, a person must consider the following core principles & strategies:

- **Self-Evaluation Audit** - Conduct a detailed weekly self-evaluation & lifestyle audit.

- **Mindset Management** - Critically think to filter and elevate using a measured response on a quest to evaluate truth on your own terms.

  o **Mindset Reset** - Remove subconscious malformed thoughts or ideation. Extract powerless programming or debilitating disempowering beliefs. Schedule time to meditate, rest & restore to emotionally clear and evoke inner peace through stillness.

  o **Mindset Map** - Analyze pre-existing paradigms that operate subconsciously in your life. Mind clearing is vital to your well-being. Do not allow negativity to consume emotional real estate in your head, the price is too high.

- **Circle of Trust** – Support systems in your life infrastructure should be lifters. Establish your trusted tribe.

- **Digital Detox** – Unplug & eliminate digital consumption to elevate.

- **Rebalanced Space** - Clutter creates a chaotic mind, decluttering lightens your load. Reduce the number of visual complexities and eliminate inefficient churning.

- **Soul Work** - Listen to your inner guidance & intuitive wisdom. Don't ever let any person, place or thing break your soul or life purpose. Never give up.

- **Outcome Expectancy** - Prioritize tasks that align with your core values & goals. Focus on adding value & positive returns.

- **Resource Allocation** – Effectively optimize and allocate your energy, time, money, & resources.

- **Trigger Evaluation** – Analyze and identify your emotional triggers to mitigate unhealthy or negative engagement. Focus on positive responses that energize you. Accept the things you can't change, while changing the things you can.

- **Results Based Thinking (RBT)** focuses on accomplishing a specific goal or task to gain maximum value for your time and effort. Consistent top performers play an A-game, and do not succumb to downward spirals, while vigorously managing their agendas with laser focus, intention, and consistent forward momentum.

- **Energy Management -** Adapt your energy levels to specific activities at set time intervals. Identify your internal or external energy drainers to conserve and reserve your energy supply. Successful people in high demand must function in a state of overflow. It is not enough to be in a state of flow, you must be in overflow to maximize exceptional potential. Living your best life is a lifestyle, not a trend.

- **Stress Management -** If you're paralyzed by indecision, perfectionism, anxiety, or depression try a 4x4 breathing exercise. Breath in for 4 seconds, then slowly exhale for 4 seconds. The navy seals routinely do this to balance oxygen and carbon dioxide in the bloodstream to stimulate relaxation.

- **Manifestation -** A visualization mental model that systematically focuses on gravitational pull in the direction of your purpose through motion and momentum to accelerated magnetic manifestation.

- **Distraction Extraction –** Focus and remove distractions that cause derailment. Your internal compass should stay laser focused on attracting what you want in life to create a magnetic effect on a reality you love.

- **Healthy Habits & Intake -** Positive productive habits and routines establish your wellness baseline. It is critical to maintain hydration and a healthy diet to reduce chronic disease and slow the aging process to avoid being biologically older than your chronological age. The National Institute of Health substantiated this. Consume conscious cuisine for high vibrational foods full of micronutrients to fuel and energize. Nutritional intake for cellular restoration is vital, along with avoiding processed foods that lead to nutrient deficiency and toxicity build up. The Mediterranean or anti-inflammatory diet is optimal for disease prevention and longevity. *Food is medicine* and your intake should be designed to bio hack your system as a modification process for high performance, focus, energy, and health.

- **Soul Foods** - Feed your mind, body, and soul for optimal living. In an era of distraction avoid unconscious consumption, whereby 1 in 3 Americans are tethered to their phones during meals. The journal of psychology and behavior found individuals on their phones during meal times consumed 15% more calories than those with distraction-free meals.

- **Lifestyle Medicine** transforms the quality of your reality and mimics the *blue zone longevity and wellbeing philosophy* that originated from where people live the longest in the world. This is based on nutritional science and timeliness social principles. The rise in lifestyle medicine is the pendulum swinging back and evidence it works.

- **Manage Expectations** - Boundaries equal a two-letter word, NO! Have an arm's length relationship with negative situations or individuals.

- **Extraction Retraction Process** - Move, find a new job, lose weight, redesign a space, change your scenery, drive a different route. If something is inhibiting your growth, identify what it is and implement the necessary changes.

- **Time & Task Management** - Outsource non-essential stress triggering tasks. Prioritize all time sensitive fast action items to complete in 10 minutes or less.

- **Proximity Planning** – Double up, arrange and streamline your schedule to avoid downtime interruption.

- **Sleep Hygiene** - Allow yourself time to relax and restore with optimal sleep cycles to maintain your circadian rhythm functions properly.

- **Cathartic Energy Release** – Do not allow your emotions to build up, find healthy outlets to release tension, shed a tear, express yourself vocally, go for a run or workout. Unprocessed emotions will result in an unhealthy suppressed immune system, body pain, chronic disease, and inflammation.

- **Flow Zone** - When you're in the flow you just know, everything aligns naturally to a heightened state of performance. You're in-sync mode paired to your activity.

- **Mood Modulation** - The journal of positive psychology found individuals who listened to upbeat music improved their mood and happiness factor within 2 weeks. I refer to this as "Lyrical Medicine", certain music creates vibrational healing within the body.

Commit to healthy habits and challenge yourself to establish a rebalanced routine to support a life you love. A rebalanced lifestyle is its own reward that pays a lifetime of dividends.

***

To contact Darcee:

Founder, CEO, Stratego Consulting International

Personal Advisor/Coach, Global Thought Leader, Best-Selling Author,

Work-Life Rebalance Authority, Leadership Advisor, Social Impact Entrepreneur

darceemcjannet.com

strategoconsulting@gmail.com

1-403-850-1970

twitter.com/strategytogo

www.linkedin.com/pub/darcee-mcjannet

facebook.com/strategoconsulting

Karl E, Fryburg

I have spent the majority of my life as a student and scholar of success and motivational training. I have attended hundreds of seminars, webinars, and trainings in my quest for a better life, and I continue to strive for personal growth and improvement on a daily basis.

Under no circumstances do I claim to be a literary scholar. You may find some grammatical errors, run-on sentences, overcapitalization, punctuation errors, and maybe even some misspellings. I, just like all of us, am only human. Please do not condemn, criticize, or complain! If you find yourself caught up in looking for my shortcomings, you may not be allowing yourself the opportunity to learn and grow.

Others have said that reading my work is like sitting across the table from me having a conversation. I do my best to write in a simple and easy-to-understand format which makes following along with the training both educational and entertaining.

My witty phrasing and sense of humor allows you, the reader, to live in the writing as you read. Thank You in advance for believing in me and purchasing this book. ENJOY!

Have a Grateful Day!!

Karl w/a "K"11

Goal Setting Success for Personal and Financial Gain

By Karl Fryburg

Please allow me a few minutes of your time to take you on a journey through the magical world of goal setting. In this brief introduction, we will cover the basics and some strategies to help create clarity around goal setting and how to be successful in the process.

Goal setting has been around for many centuries and has been traced back to the days of Aristotle and the Greek Philosophers in the early 300s B.C. In the Aristotelian Principle of General Applicability, goal setting was referred to as the "Fourth Cause" or "Final Cause." If Ancient Greek Philosophy is a path you enjoy pursuing, there is a plethora of information regarding Aristotle's Theory.

With so many distractions and interruptions in the fast-paced world we live in today, goal setting can be a challenge. If you take the time to learn about the habits and traits of the most successful people on the planet, you will find a common thread amongst them: goal setting.

There are very few major accomplishments within the course of history that did not come to fruition without clearly defined and set goals. All major roads, highways, and construction projects throughout the globe are carefully planned, coordinated, and executed with a series of completion deadlines, schedules, and strategies.

Goal setting can be as simple as setting an alarm, planning a vacation, gathering, or even making a meal. Most of us do not think of these when we think about goals and goal setting, but they all have the same characteristics regardless of size or complexity.

The majority of people today go through life creating, planning, and executing goal-setting techniques and do not even realize they are doing it. Most people do not just wake up one morning and say, "I am going to go buy a car today." They have looked at ads, read reviews, asked other car owners how they like their choice and performed various tasks to assist in their decision-making process.

Taking goal setting to a level of personal and financial success requires commitment, planning, strategies, and execution. In order to achieve true success and greatness, goal setting must become an intimate part of your daily life and routine. These are some examples of goal setting in their simplest of forms.

In the time before Google Maps, MapQuest, and GPS Navigation, there was a company (which is still around) called AAA. The American Automobile Association was your "Go To" source for planning and "mapping" out the family road trip or summer vacation. You would visit their office and sit down with a "planner" who would help you to plan your trip every step of the way.

Stay with me for a minute, as it will all reveal itself here in a moment. Your AAA "Trip Tic," as it was known, would be compiled for you and included the following:

- Road maps with yellow highlighter lines showing the exact route you were going

  to take on a daily basis to reach your final destination or "Goal."

- Recorded and calculated distances that included options for where to visit, stop

  for a view, where to eat, where you would stop for the night, and much more.

- A daily "Goal" for you to accomplish to get to each destination and inevitably

  end up at the hotel/motel in time for a swim, dinner, or just time to relax before

  the next day's travels.

Most of us remember wanting to stop to go to the bathroom or to look at some roadside attraction only to be told that it was not part of the plan. Whoever was driving was in control as a result of the careful planning and execution of the AAA plan.

I am hoping that some of you just had an "AhhhHaaa" moment while enjoying my example. Goal setting is an integral part of everyday life and can be instrumental in successfully completing a dream, vision, desire, or challenge with which you are faced. Goal setting may be the first step and, ultimately, the one procedure that any person can execute to begin a journey to great accomplishments in life, both large and small.

Setting and "road mapping" goals and realizing those goals can set you apart from the majority of the world and accelerate your personal, financial, physical, spiritual, and social life to new levels in a relatively brief period of time.

One of my favorite quotes from Brian Tracy is: "If what you are doing is not moving you towards your goals, then it's moving you away from them."

There is a vast knowledge base surrounding goal setting, clinical and real-world studies, and documentation proving that goals can accelerate your personal and financial growth and success. So many people speak of letting life happen for us rather than to us, and goal setting can play a huge role in this part of your quest, both personally and financially.

There has also been research and documentation around goal-setting theory. For those of you who like going down those types of rabbit holes, there is plenty of information out there to get your cup filled up. Edwin Locke's "Toward a Theory of Task Motivation and Incentives" (1968) and T.A. Ryan's "Intentional Behavior" (1970) are two good places to start.

The idea and concept behind Goal Setting Theory are that of having a purposeful and conscious goal which obviously will increase the likelihood that what you are focused on accomplishing will most likely come to fruition if properly planned and executed.

I am sure you are curious to learn more about how setting goals will help you to achieve the kind of life that others only wish for, so this next section will break down a few steps and processes. I also have a book with a workbook available on my website that breaks it down into "bite-sized" pieces and step-by-step exercises to help get you in the habit of creating and executing proper goal-setting practices.

Here are three principles or ideas that will help you to understand the process and set you on the path to proper goal setting.

First and foremost is Clarity! The more you specify and identify the goal you are setting for yourself, the more likely your chance of success will be.

- Saying "I want to lose weight" is vague at best and has little or no clarity.

- Saying "I want to lose 15 pounds" is better.

- Saying "I want to lose 15 pounds in the next 30 days is better, better.

- Saying "I want to lose 15 pounds in the next 30 days so that I will look great at my reunion, friend's wedding, etc. is even better and heading for the best.

Second, and equally important, is a goal with a Challenge! If you set easy goals that require little or no effort, you will succeed but most likely will not grow.

- Create goals that will require initiative, motivation, and focus. If they are too easy,

   there is no challenge and no growth.

- Create manageable goals that will create a sense of accomplishment and pride to

   help keep you engaged and satisfied with the results you obtain and allow you to

   feel good about what you are doing.

- Create a process of small steps, or goals, within the process to allow for small

   wins during the duration of the specific goal challenge.

"C" number 3. As with any task, skill, plan, goal, or process, you must make a Commitment, or failure is almost certainly going to be the outcome.

- Being Willing (having the Will) to do "Whatever it Takes" to achieve the goal/s

   you have set out to accomplish is the most important part of the process.

- Being Sincere (genuine in feeling) and taking ownership of the process and

steps required to achieve said goals are the key to your success.

- Being Motivated (incentive or strong desire) and self-regulated are also vital

parts of the commitment necessary to properly achieve your goals.

Many people will often wonder if they really need to set goals and why it is so important. The answer is YES! Goal setting can absolutely change the entire trajectory of a person's life and give them the opportunity to achieve levels of success they never knew were even possible. Goal setting comes with many challenges and many benefits. The trick is to reap the benefits and grow from the challenges.

There are many benefits that can be enjoyed with proper setting and execution of goals. Many achieve greater satisfaction and success in many aspects of their lives as a result of staying true to the process and seeing it through to the finish line.

Many have been concerned about what happens if the goal is not achieved, and I can assure you the answer to this question is simple: Reset the Goal! Without goals, we have a tendency to go through life waddling through the abyss with no drive, aim, direction, purpose, or accomplishment.

If you find that you did not complete your set goal in the time frame that you set forth, it is ok and also means that the goal may have been just a little out of reach. One of my favorite phrases is: "When you win, you win, and when you lose, you learn." Review the goal that you did not achieve and analyze the setbacks or causes of the missed goal.

You will often see exactly what was missing from the equation or what went wrong simply by looking deeper into the cause of the incompletion. I hope you have noticed by now that I have not used the words fail, failed, or failure in this writing because there is no such thing as failure in goal setting. There are only wins, accomplishments, challenges resulting in temporary setbacks, and areas of concern which need to be addressed the next time the goal is set.

These are the things that will keep you going and focused on your ultimate desire, which is the achievement of the goal. One of the best practices when setting goals and "mapping" out the journey of the goal is to create sub-goals within the goal. Some call this mind mapping, flowcharting, reverse engineering, or structuring the goal.

If you take the time to structure or map out the process from start to finish, you will greatly increase your probability of success with any and all goals. When hitting the smaller micro-goals within the process, it is also a good practice to reward yourself. We all remember the feeling as a child when the teacher, instructor, or tutor would honor us with some comment, gold star, recognition, or award as a result of our accomplishment.

Rewarding yourself for reaching certain plateaus in the larger process will not only help to keep you focused and motivated, but it will also make you feel pretty darn good about yourself. Small accomplishments equal small rewards, while large accomplishments require large rewards. The mind becomes stimulated very easily by kudos and recognition, and this stimulation creates additional motivation.

There are many primary reasons that goal setting is important and is so widely used by successful individuals worldwide, and I am going to share a few here to bring this chapter to a close.

I was going to put this off until later, but I decided to lead with "Procrastination." I do not need to give the definition of this word as I am sure you are all aware of its meaning and what it can do to your progress and success. Setting clearly defined and written goals with their appropriate timelines is one of the greatest ways to eliminate procrastination from your life and your vocabulary.

On the other side of procrastination is motivation. Goal setting has been referred to by many successful and prominent leaders throughout the globe as one of the best and simplest forms of motivation there is. Having your dreams, visions, and goals mapped out and in plain sight for you to review will help you accelerate the process and will absolutely motivate you.

As you begin to fulfill those promises you made to yourself and continue to check off the completed wins and goals, you will find a noticeable and absolute increase in your motivation. We have yet to discover time travel, but the successful execution of clearly defined and written goals with timelines and completion dates is similar to bending the space-time continuum and bridging the gap from the start to the finish of any said goal.

Goal setting will help eliminate distractions and enhance focus. I believe the majority of you reading this have, at one time or another (or daily), created a "to-do" list to help to streamline your day and get more done. This is goal setting in its simplest form. Focus becomes a lesser foe when you have a clear path set forth in front of you with your written goals and tasks.

Goal setting will shorten the gap and help you achieve more in less time. As these "Achievements" unfold, you will find that all of the practices and processes within the process will continually become less challenging and more exciting as you grow your goal-setting system and work out the bugs. You will also find, as you continue to grow and expand, that your progress will become more measurable.

"A Journey of a thousand miles begins with the first step" - Lao Tzu.

Having clearly defined and written goals will also help you to determine what you want in life with more clarity. It is a known fact that the top income earners and most successful people in the world all have a common thread: Goal Setting.

As I bring this writing to a close, I will also be rewarding myself for completing another goal. I received notification that this publication was finalized, and it was time to submit our chapter for insertion and printing. There was a deadline that had to be met, and my schedule was pretty full.

The beauty of successful goal setting is that all goals are not cast in stone. Everything can be changed and modified as needed to allow for the unexpected, provided that you do not get too far off track. With a few shifts and omissions, I was able to insert this project into my flow and complete this writing with several days to go so that it could be reviewed and edited before the deadline.

I wish to leave you all with an exercise in imagination that I think will wrap this up with a nice bow. Take a moment and think back to your childhood when we all said, "When I grow up, I want to be . . . ." If you were one of those "Dreamers," it is most likely that life got in the way and what you had imagined did not turn into reality. If you achieved those Dreams, Goals, and Visions, I congratulate you!

Here is the exercise:

- I just wrote you a check for $1,000,000.00!

- It's yours to do with as you please!

- Take no more than 5 minutes with a clean piece of paper and write down 10

  things you would do with your newfound Million Dollars!

- Leave a couple of spaces on the paper between each of these ten things

- Don't get caught up in it, and just DO IT! NOW! (see you in 5 minutes)

If you thought this exercise was silly and did not do the exercise, there is no need to continue reading.

If you actually did the exercise, a Miracle has just occurred!

You have just written a list of Personal, Financial, and/or Spiritual Growth goals!

The "Million Dollar Question is:

"Why have I not pursued these Dreams, Visions, and Goals before?"

Go back and take a look at what you wrote down and use the empty spaces to jot down what you think it will take to achieve these things without the Million Dollars. You will be surprised at how you can actually see that there is a possibility that you may be able to achieve these goals without the money.

I hope that many of you have just had another AhhhHaaa moment, and you begin looking at life through a different set of eyes than you had a little bit ago when you began reading my ramblings.

If you have made it this far, I would Love to congratulate you for being a candidate for the top 1 to 3% of successful people in the world!

***

Please feel free to reach out to me at
www.runningforyourlifestyle.com

or find me on Facebook @
https://www.facebook.com/karl.fryburg/

Have a Grateful Day!!

Karl w/a "K"!

Dr. Patricia Rogers

Dr. Rogers is a business coach and event coordinator well-versed in today's technology and systems. She uses her expertise to coach entrepreneurs on using the systems that will grow their businesses.

She hosts and organizes annual virtual events that set a platform for entrepreneurs to speak and promote their products. Dr. Rogers gives you exposure through LIVE interviews and teaches you how to build relationships across social platforms.

Dr. Rogers is the Head of Theophany University in Haiti, allowing her to recommend you for the *"Honorary of Doctor Award"* for completed work and service.

CEO of Unity In Service, Inc., a retired Corrections Lieutenant with 29 years in law enforcement, trained thousands of employees to excel in their careers. A 12-year veteran of the US Army & Graduate of ST. Thomas University.

She has positioned herself as a Visibility Strategist| 2xTime Winning International Public Speaker | International Best-Selling Author| Business Coach & Virtual Event Coordinator.

Her *"Inspirational Breakthrough System"* will show you strategies, improve your personal development, and build confidence. Visit: PatriciaRogers.com/System/

She is the recipient of many awards and has appeared in many magazines.

Quitting Is Never an Option

By Dr. Patricia Rogers

The rewards are great when we realize how invaluable people are. If you want to grow your network, whether via email, phone, social media, radio, podcast, or even virtual events. I encourage you to make networking a part of your agenda.

When you decide to host your event, I encourage you to network virtually and in-person as much as possible. Hosting events builds your email list of individuals who share your passion for connecting with others. It has been a fantastic journey since I discovered my gifts, talents, and hobbies and turned them into a business. I want to support you in your desire to host useful networking events that educate and inspire others. I want to share with you what I went through that assisted me in discovering my true purpose.

If you are already hosting events, I am sure you will be able to learn even more tips, strategies, and processes when you connect with me or be a speaker at the virtual events that we host. Visit: Calendly.com/PatRogers/

If you plan to be a connector for other people, you have made a wise investment in purchasing this book. According to Napoleon Hill in *Think and Grow Rich*, "One sound idea is all you need to succeed!" If you enjoy being around people and love bringing people together for whatever reason, you may have a gift or talent you can turn into a business.

Networking is big business today. Although we have been networking for centuries, people coming together was only sometimes called networking. The word entered English in the 1550s to mean anything formed by presenting the appearance of a net or netting. By 1972, it was applied to computers. In 1982, the word networking became a verb. Referring to interacting with others to exchange information and develop contacts.

Networking is when a group gets together for a common cause to achieve a desired result using collaboration and exchanging or sharing ideas, products, or services to enhance other people's lifestyles.

The Merriam-Webster online dictionary defines networking as "The exchange of information or services among individuals, groups, or institutions specifically: the cultivation of productive relationships for employment or business."

Both definitions are on point as they require people to come together. While preparing for the corporal examination for my promotion in Corporate America, I remember reading from a book, *Supervisory Management*, Chapter 8, *"Getting Results Through People."* I will never forget what I read: "People are our best resources." That stayed with me. Looking over your life at your achievements and challenges, other people were always involved.

Since retiring in two thousand sixteen, I have met the best of the best, sat with the cream of the crop, and been mentored by the rich and the famous. If I had not pushed through the fears of the unknown, changed my mindset, and "got up, suited up, and showed up," I would have missed so much. Success does not find you; you must find it. Where do we look for success? *In other people.*

Correctional Officer to CEO

Here is a bit about my story and why I have chosen to discover my gifts and hobbies and turn them into a business I love. Are you aware of **politics in the**

workplace?

During my law enforcement career, I achieved many accolades, but I also faced feelings of fear, inadequacy, and unappreciation. Early in my career, I learned that when you know what you want, you will work hard to achieve it, and no matter what distractions show up, there will be a drive within you that will not allow you to lose sight of your goal. Everyone has rights, but you need to know your rights to have them.

About eight years into my career, I decided to take the examination for the first level of supervision. As I was studying the policies and procedures for the promotional exam, I learned that employees had rights. I also learned that there were procedures that employees must adhere to if they wanted to file complaints.

What I did was different from the rules. I went before the Board of County Commissioners on national television to plead my case. It was different from the standard. It was an opportunity that presented itself, and I took advantage of it. I wanted someone who had the power to change the narrative of my situation at the time. I had already filed grievances and personnel complaints, and this was an added opportunity for me to be heard. I persevered, and I succeeded.

The county commissioners instructed the department administrators to get it right, and I was promoted with back pay.

Two years later, I took the exam for the second level of supervision. I am sure you can attest that you become a target when you stand up for what's right. By now, I had become a bigger target for making the first complaint. Getting over your fears is the key to reaching your goals. You must face the fear head-on, knowing that what you want is waiting on the other side of the fear.

I took the test, passed it, and came out in the top ten percentile. Again, management skipped over me for the promotion. I knew my rights, so I challenged the decision administratively again and was promoted.

My goal was to retire as a Correctional Lieutenant, and because I was nearing my retirement, I decided to take the lieutenant's exam. However, I was overcome with the fear of being passed over by now. I persevered, overcame my anxiety, and when I took the test, I came out in the top five percentile. Guess what happened? Yep, you got it; they denied me the promotion.

Did they think they could hold me down, bypassing me for promotions? I oversaw male inmates with 200lb biceps at various jails who worked out daily pumping iron. I supervised male and female inmates charged with rape, robbery, kidnapping, and murder. I guarded these inmates for years, and management thought they could hold me down by not giving me my promotion!

I want you to remember this when people try to defeat you and even when you are working against yourself. "With every success comes challenges and hard work, but when you face each difficulty and overcome them, they should move you into a space that inspires you to achieve even more success." Quitting is never an option.

I retired as a corrections lieutenant in two thousand sixteen from Miami-Dade County Corrections. Today, the Florida Retirement System pays me a six-figure salary plus a three percent annual increase for the remainder of my life. Keeping your eyes on the prize is crucial in reaching your goal.

Before retiring, I knew preparation was the key to a productive retirement. Retirement would allow me to discover my gifts, talents, and hobbies. When working for corporate America, you do not have to know the gifts inside of you that you can monetize. You only have to go to work, read the policies and procedures that are in place, and do what you are told to do.

Your Gifts Make Room for You

When going through challenges, focus on the positive, and you will get through the challenge. While I had been bypassed for the second promotion, I noticed that employees who wanted to excel in their careers kept coming to me for assistance in preparing for promotional examinations. Then, I remembered that the questions I had created from each policy and procedure could teach others how to study for the examinations. So, I began putting together notebooks with the questions I had created. I began to sell the notebooks of the questions for each policy, and the employees would purchase the notebooks from me.

While I was going through my battle fighting for my promotion, I also started teaching employees at the community library how to take the promotional exam. People were watching me, and even through my struggles, people were counting on me. I assisted many employees in reaching the next level in their careers. When you give to others, it comes back to you because your gift makes room for you to be an asset to others. When you focus on others, you do not have to focus on the difficulties that you may be facing.

I have always been a leader and outspoken for good reasons—even the things I learned during the challenging times in my youth and the years spent in the U.S. Army, law enforcement, and even my youth prepared me for my successful journey. They all contributed to where God was going to take me.

Preparation Is the Key To Success

Before retiring, I joined a multilevel company called LegalShield. I fell in love with the services because I encountered a vast amount of injustice in the workplace. I also learned that when your rights are being violated, you have to consult with the experts in the legal arena, so marketing legal and identity theft services were up my alley. I attended networking events as a sponsored vendor and protected many families with the necessary legal protection. I received many bonuses for the families, business owners, and individuals who invested in the services of LegalShield. I was laying the foundation to ensure I did not return to the corporate arena again.

While still working in the corporate arena, I started hosting networking events in my backyard to market my legal services—other entrepreneurs were invited to attend and share their products and services by sharing a sixty-second infomercial. I paid for the DJ and food, rented tables and chairs for the vendors, and fifty to sixty people would be in my backyard.

I did lots of networking to learn what entrepreneurs were doing. I invested in coaches Bill Walsh, a Small Business Expert, Nancy Matthews, Women's Prosperity Network co-founder, and Sharon Lechter, author of Think & Grow Rich for Women. I only wanted to learn more strategies to make more sales in my LegalShield business.

As fate would have it, each coach stated, "You already have a business if you are hosting events in your backyard, and all you have to do is monetize your events.

With the education and training of my mentors, I learned to turn my passion into a business I love.

My passion has always been to be around people. I enjoy sharing my thoughts on open forums and creating ways to unite people. My "people personality" led me into the role of an event coordinator, which is my zone of genius, and I learned that once when I invested in coaches. I learned that connecting with people was a hobby, and when I identified that as one of my gifts, the next step was to monetize.

My Zone of Genius

I was approaching my retirement date and another opportunity to throw a big party. I wanted to create a memorable experience, so I hired a horse-drawn carriage and arrived at the site to the jubilant sounds of horns. It was a momentous event that started my new life as an entrepreneur.

I monetized my gifts. For seven years, I went into the most elegant hotels hosting conferences that bring entrepreneurs together to create even more wealth while providing solutions through the use of the resources they provide! *"People Need People,"* and groundwork is the key to success!

My events and conferences grew exponentially, and after investing in myself and being mentored, I became an even more successful entrepreneur. As the founder of Unity in Service, Inc., I positioned myself as a Business Development Strategist, Best-Selling Author, Social Media Marketer, and Public Speaker.

My passion is teaching, inspiring, and providing a stage for entrepreneurs to share their message at our live conferences. Expert Panelists respond to questions the event moderator asks, and the vendors display their products and services, each while building relationships and creating even more wealth!

The Big Conference

In May 2020, we had the most significant conference planned, with over seventy participants, including speakers, expert panelists, sponsored vendors, and volunteers. Each participant had invested in their role in the event, and we were anxious to get the ticket sales started.

We were well into the profit mode and looking forward to more sales when we set up our Eventbrite to sell tickets to the hundreds of expected attendees.

Everything was well underway by now, and it was time for the out-of-town participants to make their flight reservations to attend the annual conference. Yes, we had arrived!

The Pandemic Shock?

Have you ever completed your plan and been hit with an unexpected challenge? Ihave had my share on many occasions in life, and if you have not experienced any, trust me, you will. I will share how I managed when the two-by-four pandemic blindsided me.

On March 20, 2020, we learned that the pandemic had hit home. It was no longer just in other countries, Italy, Japan, and Africa, but was now in our backyard, the United States. Then it got closer and began affecting people within a 100-mile radius of where I lived.

I was contacted by Eventbrite, who advised me that I had to cancel or postpone the May 2020 event due to the pandemic. Then, the hotel where the big conference was scheduled called me and told me we would refund the security deposit we paid to secure the conference rooms. **COVID-19** changed my life, and the effects of it blindsided me and shook me into a haze of fear and uncertainty.

I doubted that it was real at first. I hoped that it would blow over and all would be normal. I had a huge conference lined up for May 2020. Unfortunately, I knew this epidemic was real within a couple of weeks of its inception, and before I knew it, the entire nation was on lockdown.

My dreams of hosting my big conference had gone up in smoke. The pandemic was now affecting my livelihood. Before the news about the widespread epidemic, many other entrepreneurs had already scheduled in-person live conferences. Now that the pandemic attacked us, all live events stopped.

Where Do I Go from Here?

Be creative and discover new gifts that you possess. **COVID-19** brought out the best in me and made me step out of my comfort zone.

Before the pandemic, I was an "Event Coordinator." **COVID-19** sent me in a new direction. I had to make a pivot, and I had to do it quickly.

My Coach, Nancy Matthews, Founder of Women's Prosperity Network, brought the organization members together in our first online coaching sessions since the pandemic shock. Her first message was to accept that things are different, and she advised us to maintain our vision to serve. She suggested that we make the *pivot* in a new direction to allow our dreams to stay alive.

I did not want my dream to die inside of me, so I took swift action. I took Coach Nancy's advice and started discovering the hidden treasures within me. I started self-training on how to conduct **"online events."**

I mastered the challenge that threatened me, and in a four (5) month period, I hosted over seven (7) online events, seating from 50 to 100 attendees. One of my mentors used to say, *"You cannotstop a man or woman who will not quit."*

Change is inevitable, and today, I am your **"Visibility Strategist." 2x Winning Public Speaker| International Best-Selling Author, Event Coordinator & Host| Business Coach and** I teach entrepreneurs how to show up professionally using technology and social media presence, which allows them to overcome their fears and gain visibility for their brands on social media platforms.

I have hosted over forty virtual events and coached others to do the same. I was appointed "Head of Relations" for Theophany University in Haiti—another amazing door of opportunity due to the pandemic. I recommend entrepreneurs for the Honorary Doctorate of Humanity Award, which allows them to add the title **"Dr"** to their names for the services and life experiences they have already done. Schedule @ Calendly.com/PatRogers

Our virtual events are thriving; they open doors of opportunity for public speakers to speak and build profitable relationships that increase their bottom lines. I host a podcast, **"Spotlights On You,"** interviewing entrepreneurs for more exposure.

R.S.V.P. Here: https://bit.ly/EnhancingYourBrand

Through unexpected crises and the challenges, I endured in my career, I discovered new gifts inside of me and learned that *"Fear is the seasoning that gives success its flavor."*

Today, I am living life on my own terms! "Preparation was the Key" to retire in style, and *"People Need People"* to thrive and to share their victories!"

***

To contact Dr. Rogers:

Website: PatriciaRogers.com (Complimentary Gift)

Email: Info@PatriciaRogers.com

All Media Sites: PatriciaRogers360.com

Nicole Harvick

Nicole Harvick is known as The Quantum Energy Healer and Forgiveness Expert because she can help you find and release old traumas that are stuck in your body. An example of what she has achieved is helping a 55-year-old woman find the exact moment she felt unworthy and unloved. The woman was just 18 months old when the trauma occurred.

Her passion is forgiveness, and she is now on a mission to help others understand and practice forgiveness in their own lives. Her desire is to help as many people as possible to utilize forgiveness to help them walk their path free of any negative emotions or pain that resides in their body.

Nicole is certified in many healing modalities including Usui Reiki, Tuning Fork Therapy, Quantum Energy Healing and is a certified Ho'oponopono EFT Practitioner.

She is also certified to facilitate meditation and does that both in person and online.

Nicole is the designer and creator of The Ho"oponopono Bracelet.® This is a line of both men and women's bracelets which are infused with reiki energy, prayer and sound.

Nicole the is the author of several books including,

Boy on a Swing" 2018

The Gift of Forgiveness 2019

The Alchemy of Forgiveness 2021

1% More 2022

Nicole resides in South Carolina where she enjoys days at the beach along with kayaking, paddleboarding, yoga and meditation.

Living Beyond the 3rd Dimension

By Nicole Harvick

My journey of spirituality started for me as a child. I did not really understand what spirituality or spirits were, but I often had vivid dreams in which I was being strangled. I once woke up and was pulling something off my throat. I held seances as a child. I read every book I could find about the spirit world. As I reflect, I now know this was always my path to walk.

I have always had Clair abilities, with my strongest being Clairaudient, which is the ability to hear and receive messages.

When I started writing the chapter for this book, I was going to write about forgiveness and self-love. This is a subject that I write, teach, and speak about. However, as I neared the completion of my chapter, I received a message from my spirit guides. They said to me, Same Content, Same Outcome.

Knowing this was a message, I asked them what they wanted me to write about. The answer was that they were asking me to write about my journey from existing in a 3rd-dimensional reality to thriving in a 5th-dimensional timeline. I always know it's best to listen to my guides and intuition.

Let's begin with an explanation of what the 3rd dimension is.

Living in a 3rd-dimensional reality can be challenging to comprehend, especially if unfamiliar with the concept. The third dimension is the physical plane of existence, characterized by length, width, and height. It is the reality we experience in our daily lives, and most people believe this to be the only reality that exists. However, a few signs indicate when we are living in a 3rd-dimensional reality.

Firstly, the sense of separation is a sign of living in a 3rd-dimensional reality. This separation is often a feeling of disconnection from others, nature, and the universe. People living in a 3rd-dimensional reality typically feel alone in an unresponsive world. They feel that everything is separate from them, and they have difficulty seeing how everything is connected.

Another sign of living in a 3rd-dimensional reality is a focus on physicality. In this reality, physicality is seen as the only reality, and everything is judged based on physical appearance. People living in a 3rd-dimensional world often judge others based on their physical appearance, believing that the physical world is all there is to life. This attitude often leads to a lack of spiritual growth and personal development, as they fail to see beyond the physical.

A third sign of living in a 3rd-dimensional reality is a belief in linear time. The notion of time is seen as something that can never be changed, and everything is expected to progress linearly and predictably. People believe that time is something that is fixed, and nothing can be done to alter it. This belief often leads to a rigid mindset, where people refuse to consider that there are other ways of viewing time.

Finally, focusing on material wealth signifies living in a 3rd-dimensional reality. People often believe having money and material possessions is the key to happiness and success. As a result, they are often obsessed with acquiring more things and competing with others in a never-ending cycle of accumulation. Unfortunately, this attitude often causes people to neglect other areas of their lives, such as relationships, spirituality, and personal growth. These signs often lead to an unfulfilling life where people cannot see beyond the physical world.

Several energy blocks can occur in this frequency; one of them is the ego. This seems to be the one thing many people will fight to hold onto.

Transcending the ego is a topic that has interested spiritual seekers and thinkers throughout history. The ego is our sense of self, identity, thoughts, and emotions. It is the lens through which we experience the world. However, it can also be a source of suffering, causing us to become attached to our thoughts, feelings, and gains or losses.

Therefore, transcending the ego means letting go of these attachments and experiencing a sense of freedom and peace that goes beyond the ego.

In a 3rd dimensional reality, ego can play a significant role in how people interact with each other. It can cause them to become defensive, competitive, and even hostile towards each other. This can result in a lack of cooperation and collaboration, making it more difficult to achieve common goals.

Moreover, ego can also impact one's perception of reality. People with high levels of ego are often fixed in their ideas and beliefs, making it difficult for them to consider other perspectives. This can lead to an inability to adapt to changing circumstances and resistance to new experiences and knowledge.

The first step in transcending the ego is to become aware of it. We need to learn to recognize the ego's voice, which often encourages us to maintain our sense of self and identify with our desires, fears, and insecurities. This means we must be mindful of our thoughts, feelings, and reactions and acknowledge them without judgment. This self-awareness enables us to separate ourselves from our ego and observe it objectively.

The next step is to question the ego's assumptions. We need to ask ourselves if our beliefs and desires are necessary or if they are the product of conditioning, desires, or fear. For example, we may feel that we are not good enough unless we achieve a certain status or have a certain amount of money. However, this belief may not reflect reality and only create unnecessary suffering. We can free ourselves from our assumptions and beliefs and experience a sense of liberation by questioning our assumptions and beliefs.

Transcending the ego requires self-awareness, questioning assumptions, and developing compassion and empathy. It is a process that cannot be achieved overnight but requires consistent effort and practice. However, the rewards of transcending the ego are worth it - we can experience a sense of connectedness with others and a deep sense of inner peace that goes beyond the limitations of the ego.

Another problematic area in the 3rd dimension is alcohol.

Alcohol is a popular and socially acceptable substance that is widely consumed around the world. Many people enjoy drinking alcohol to relax, socialize, or simply have a good time. However, few realize alcohol can lower their vibrations and negatively impact their spiritual, emotional, and physical well-being.

When we talk about vibration, we refer to the energy surrounding and flowing through our bodies. Many internal and external factors influence this energy, including our thoughts, emotions, actions, and environment. Maintaining a high vibration is widely believed to be essential to living a healthy, happy, and fulfilling life.

Alcohol consumption is known to have several adverse effects on our vibration. First and foremost, alcohol is a depressant. It slows down our body's functions, including our heart rate, respiratory rate, and brain activity. This can lead to feelings of drowsiness, lethargy, and even depression.

Also, alcohol has a detrimental effect on our moods and emotions. It is known to alter our brain chemistry, impairing our ability to think clearly, feel positive emotions, and regulate our behavior which can lead to feelings of anger, aggression, anxiety, and depression.

In addition to affecting our emotions and mood, alcohol can also physically affect our bodies. Consuming an excessive amount of alcohol can cause dehydration, which can lead to fatigue, headaches, and muscle weakness. Alcohol can also damage our liver, kidneys, and other organs, leading to long-term health problems and a weaker immune system.

Perhaps most significantly, alcohol consumption can impact our spiritual vibration. Many spiritual traditions believe that we are connected to a higher power and that this connection is necessary for our spiritual growth and well-being. However, alcohol consumption can block this connection, making it more difficult for us to access our higher selves, our intuition, and our connection to the universe.

While alcohol may seem like a harmless way to have fun or unwind, it can have profound negative effects on our vibration. By lowering our mood, impairing our physical and mental health, and blocking our spiritual connection, alcohol can negatively impact our overall well-being. If you choose to consume alcohol, it is essential to do so in moderation and with awareness to avoid the negative effects that come with excessive consumption.

Now that we have uncovered some of the blocks to accession, let's talk about what enhances our soul and helps our vibration to rise. This is my favorite subject.

Forgiveness is a powerful tool that can help you prepare to live in the 5th dimension. The 5th dimension represents a state of consciousness where love, peace, harmony, and unity prevail. It is a higher state of being where you escape the limitations of time, space, and the material world. To reach this state of being, forgiveness plays a crucial role.

Forgiveness is the process of letting go of anger, resentment, blame, and other negative emotions toward oneself or others. It is a conscious choice to release the past and move forward with a new perspective and a renewed sense of peace. Forgiveness is not forgetting or condoning the past but choosing not to dwell on it or let it define your present and future.

To live in the 5th dimension, you must let go of the old patterns and belief systems that no longer serve you. These beliefs and patterns may have been ingrained in you for years and may have caused you deep pain and suffering. Forgiveness helps you break free from these patterns and beliefs, allowing you to experience a new sense of freedom and joy.

Forgiveness also allows you to speak your truth without holding onto anger or resentment. When you forgive, you let go of the need to be right and instead focus on finding a resolution that benefits everyone. This is an essential component of living in the 5th dimension, where compassion and understanding are the primary values.

Moreover, forgiveness allows you to connect with others on a deep level, creating stronger bonds of love, trust, and understanding. In the 5th dimension, relationships are based on mutual respect, empathy, and unconditional love. Forgiveness helps us see beyond our differences and connect with each other at a soul level.

Finally, forgiveness is an essential aspect of self-care. When we forgive ourselves and others, we heal emotional wounds that block our ability to love and be loved. We release the negative energy trapped in our bodies, allowing us to experience greater levels of joy, peace, and clarity.

Forgiveness plays a vital role in helping us prepare to live in the 5th dimension. It liberates us from the limitations of the past, allowing us to embrace a new level of consciousness and connect with the collective energy of love, peace, and harmony. Forgiveness is not just an act of kindness towards others but an essential aspect of our spiritual growth and evolution.

How does forgiveness lead to Self-Love?

Self-love is essential for an individual's overall well-being and happiness. It is the foundation of positive mental health, allowing us to build healthy relationships with others and be content in our skin. Forgiving oneself is an essential aspect of self-love. We often hold onto past mistakes or regrets, which can lead to negative self-talk and a sense of self-doubt. Forgiveness allows us to accept our mistakes and learn from them rather than dwelling on them and continuing to criticize ourselves.

Forgiving oneself also involves letting go of any negative emotions we may hold towards ourselves. When we forgive ourselves, we release ourselves from self-criticism and judgment, which can be incredibly freeing. This helps us cultivate a greater sense of self-compassion and self-love, allowing us to be more forgiving toward others. This is crucial to raise your vibration and to help you ascend to the 5th dimension.

Forgiveness is a critical aspect of self-love. It lets us release negative emotions and move forward into a brighter, happier future. Forgiving oneself involves accepting and learning from our mistakes, allowing us to cultivate more self-compassion and self-love. When we forgive ourselves, we open ourselves up to the possibility of growth and positive change. Embracing forgiveness can help us to become better versions of ourselves and to lead more meaningful, fulfilling lives.

Are you ready for the Fifth Dimension?

One aspect of the fifth dimension is its association with higher consciousness and spiritual awakening. Many spiritual traditions believe that accessing the fifth dimension requires a shift in perception and deepening of one's spiritual practice. It is said to be a realm of expanded awareness where one can connect with higher levels of being and access greater wisdom and insight.

Also, the 5th dimension is considered a place of infinite possibilities and manifestations. In this realm, one can experience a heightened sense of creativity and the ability to manifest one's desires with ease. This may be linked to the idea that thought and intention have a much greater impact on reality in the fifth dimension than in our three-dimensional world.

Finally, the 5th dimension is sometimes associated with the concept of unity consciousness. This refers to a state of being in which one recognizes the interconnectedness of all things and experiences a deep sense of oneness with the universe. By entering this state of consciousness, one can transcend the limitations of the ego and experience a sense of interdependence and interconnectedness with all of creation.

The 5th dimension is a complex and multifaceted concept that touches on many different aspects of human experience. While much about this dimension remains a mystery, scientific research and spiritual traditions suggest that it is a real and important phenomenon with great potential for personal growth and transformation. As we continue to explore the mysteries of the fifth dimension, we may discover new insights into the nature of reality and the meaning of our existence.

Living in the 5th dimension offers a new level of consciousness and understanding. We exist in a state of oneness, where our individuality is transcended, and our interconnectedness is celebrated. Our lives are filled with infinite possibilities as we expand our understanding of what is truly possible.

In conclusion, Many people claim to have had experiences in the 5th dimension, which is also known as the astral plane or the spiritual dimension. This dimension is said to exist beyond the physical world and is a realm of higher consciousness where beings have access to higher levels of knowledge and wisdom. Let's explore some of the experiences of a 5th-dimensional existence.

One of the most common experiences people report is feeling "lifted up" or "expanded" beyond their physical body. For me, I feel that my etheric field is greatly expanded, which gives me heightened awareness. Many, including myself, who have experienced this state often describe a sense of peace, love, joy, and a feeling of connectedness to everything around them.

Another experience often reported in the 5th dimension is the ability to communicate in a higher realm. My spirit guides speak to me through meditation or when I spend time in silence. They communicate to provide guidance, comfort or simply to offer a message of love and support. I have also encountered beings from other dimensions or realms, such as extraterrestrial and interdimensional beings. This, too, was during meditation.

I have also experienced a heightened sense of intuition and psychic abilities, including the ability to see and perceive energy, telepathy, clairvoyance, and other forms of extrasensory perception. I could also access information beyond time and space, including past lives.

The 5th dimension offers harmony and unity with all of Mother Earth's creations. This includes a deep understanding of the interconnectedness of all things and a profound respect for the natural world. I now feel a sense of responsibility to help others and work towards improving humanity.

My personal experiences include the following:

The download of messages from my guides.

Timeline Hopping

Astral Travel

Receiving information while practicing quantum healing on my clients

Ability to see energy and work on animals.

Experience and work through a vortex

While the idea of a 5th-dimensional life may seem far-fetched to some, I can tell you that my awakening and transition have been nothing short of miraculous. To live in a consciousness of kindness and joy is amazing. I can experience the love of self and the love of others, including Mother Earth and her occupants. This is a path of great knowledge and wisdom. This is a path to truly be of service to others.

Those of us who were blessed with these amazing gifts have also agreed to share them with others for the benefit of humanity. It is truly a wonderful journey, and I am honored to be able to be here to serve and assist mankind.

***

To contact Nicole:

https://www.facebook.com/nicole.harvick.90/

https://www.instagram.com/nicolesharvick/

(1) Nicole Harvick | LinkedIn

www.nicoleharvick.com

nicoleharvick@gmail.com

My Calendly - Event Types - Calendly

Deana Brown Mitchell

Deana Brown Mitchell is a driven, optimistic, and compassionate leader in all areas of her life.

As a bestselling author, speaker and award-winning entrepreneur, Deana vulnerably shares her experiences for the benefit of others. As a consultant, she has a unique perspective on customizing a path forward for any situation.

Currently President of Genius & Sanity, and known as **"The Shower Genius"**, she teaches her proprietary framework created from her own experiences of burnout and always putting herself last... for entrepreneurs and leaders who want to continue or expand their business while taking better care of themselves and achieving the life of their dreams.

In 2022 Deana released the book, *The Shower Genius, How Self-Care, Creativity & Sanity will Change Your Life Personally & Professionally.*

Also, Deana is the Founder & Executive Director of The Realize Foundation. She is a suicide survivor herself, and vulnerably uses her own mental health journey to let others know there is hope. The Realize Foundation produces events and publishes books that let people know there are not alone.

"But I will restore you to health and heal your wounds" Jeremiah 30:17

Thankful for the Scars

By Deana Brown Mitchell

Definition of SCAR: a feeling of great emotional pain or sadness that is caused by a bad experience and lasts a long time.

Google says... A scar always represents pain endured. Pain is part of what it means to be human, and scars become silent proof of that humanity. For some, scars symbolize that life is full of pain and suffering that must be endured with strength and stoicism.

In our life, there is one thing for certain, there will always be challenges, trouble, and hard times. Some will be small and forgettable, some will be breathtaking and long lasting, some will leave permanent marks, and some are necessary to get us to the next level. These events in our lives are often hard to bear, depressing or suppressing; but there is always a lesson. The takeaway might be a tangible lesson about not leaving your door unlocked, or it could be more along the lines of the consequences for not taking care of ourselves, physically or mentally. Neglect of a child or an animal is a crime, but neglecting ourselves is something we cannot blame on anyone else.

We must take life's challenges as they come and decide individually how we will deal with them. Will you stand up and take them head on, addressing your mental capacity along the way? Or might you stuff it down and turn to addiction to hide the pain? We all have these choices, but we are all equipped at different levels to handle these challenges based on our unique life experiences.

No matter how we may be equipped to handle what life throws at us, the hard times are inevitable. Some of them may debilitate us in a way that our life is never the same. Some of them may be a lesson that makes our experiences in the future better because of it. Maybe it is something minor, but we learn from it. They happen to every single one of us.

I call them scars...

Scars can keep us silent, in shame and feeling small where the pain seems to go on forever. If we take the time to acknowledge the pain, process the journey in a healthy way and heal from the obstacle, we can turn them into an incredible message, movement, and/or success. This can bring us purpose, and it can bring healing to others that hear your story and realize they are not alone.

Some scars are a physical mark on your body that remind you of a painful time, like cutting your knee and getting stitches or a traumatic injury of some sort. Other scars may be invisible to everyone else, but are much deeper and emotional, possibly from abuse or a relationship.

Sometimes we wear scars as a badge of honor, so we can look tough or feel strong for surviving. I always thought that my physical scars were stronger than our regular skin, almost like a superpower. Feeling like I could not be hurt again in that same way because I was invincible from the original trauma. After some research on this, there are differing opinions for sure about scar tissue versus skin, but I stick by my statement that scars make us stronger and wiser if we allow it. They make us stronger physically in some instances, but always mentally, if we address the pain and heal from it.

"Owning our story can be hard, but not nearly as difficult as spending our lives running from it. Embracing our vulnerabilities is risky, but not nearly as dangerous as giving up on love and belonging and joy—the experiences that make us the most vulnerable. Only when we are brave enough to explore the darkness will we discover the infinite power of our light."

~ Brene Brown

It was May of 1997, the week of Cinco de Mayo in Phoenix, Arizona. At the time I was a manager at a local Mexican restaurant, and I was in a not-so-healthy relationship.

It was my 27th year in this life and I was ready to be done with it.

Fortunately, God had other plans for me, but when I woke up in the hospital, I was angry and could not see past the moment. I was in the middle of the biggest scar of my young life. I could not understand how or why I survived. When the nurse told me, *"You are lucky to be alive"*, I am sure I was visibly irritated. I did not understand why I was saved from my self-inflictions.

Decades later, I was on the phone with a friend and colleague answering questions about another friend and colleague that had left the organization. At the time I was running my event/Destination Management Company and worked with both and their clients. When I told the friend on the call that the other friend and I had been trying to get together for months to have lunch, he got quiet and whispered, *"you don't know…"*

Immediately my heart sank, I had to catch my breath. My friend felt similar to how I felt all those years earlier, but he succeeded in what I couldn't.

I knew he was struggling and that is why we were trying to get together, but he had no idea about my past. I was grieving the loss of this person I knew for twenty plus years and God was using this event to insert my true calling and purpose in my life. You see, I had never spoken to anyone about my failed suicide attempt, but my thoughts were swirling with *"what if my friend knew my story"*, *"could I have helped"*, *"would they still be here"*?

My Lord and Savior Jesus Christ, who miraculously saved me so many years earlier, was letting me know that I needed to speak up. My initial thought was, *"you want me to do what!?!"* I could not possibly fathom telling anyone about this darkest deepest secret… what about my clients, my employees, my family?

The one thing that kept pushing me was losing my friend and wondering if I could have helped. I was terrified that I would ever be in that position again. So, I had to be vulnerable about the worst moment of my life in order to let others know that they are not alone.

"Authenticity is a collection of choices that we must make every day. It's about the choice to show up and be real. The choice to be honest. The choice to let our true selves be seen."

~ Brene Brown

After stewing on this for months, I finally decided to tell my story publicly, start a non-profit, and do what I was being called to do. Making the decision and actually doing it was two different things! On January 28, 2020, I was turning fifty. I took this opportunity to set my new mission in stone, I needed to commemorate this decision in a way that I could not back out of it. The shame was not going to stop me this time. I got the words *"Thankful for the Scars"* tattooed on my forearm. Now, every time I look down, I am reminded of my journey, my friend's passing, and my commitment to help others know there is hope.

I am also reminded of the twenty-three years silence. I never talked about it, never sought help, never processed the journey, and never fully healed. During those decades, there was never an advertisement, and organization, a situation or a conversation that ever made me feel like it was ok to talk about the fact that I had tried to end my life.

There were tons of resources when I actually looked for them. I spent hours, days and months during the COVID-19 shutdown researching suicide and everything I could find about mental health. When I finally met another suicide survivor, I no longer felt alone. And I talked about it more and more.

I would be remiss if I did not mention the song, "SCARS" by I Am They. My entire attitude, approach, and the words in this chapter you are reading came from what I learned in that song. It gave me the perspective that is the basis of what I have presented to you here. Scars are lessons, steppingstones to our next victory, our next purpose, and to the wisdom, kindness and healing we can pass on to humanity.

"Whatever you can conceive and believe, you can achieve."

~ Napoleon Hill

Between getting the permanent words on my arm and March 2020 when the whole world shut down; I was running my multi-million-dollar business. I was making sure to wear long sleeves, as I was not ready to answer questions about the new ink. People close to me knew that I was talking about suicide in the context of losing a dear friend, but they still did not know the whole story.

Our business forecast for the year was double our best year ever in revenue. My team and I were talking about the new non-profit being a give back part of the business in the sense that we would create team building/Corporate Social Responsibility events around mental health awareness. We were in the brainstorming phase when the pandemic shut everything down.

Due to the fact that we did logistics for corporate incentive travel all over the state of Colorado, we lost multiple 7-figures within the month. A few months later I closed the business, filed for bankruptcy, and lost everything. The kicker was that June 2020 would have been out 10th anniversary and our best year ever. I was devastated.

I just did not have a vision of what I had to offer in the mental health arena. There were so many people in the world with Psychology degrees and I felt they were more equipped than me to address the issue of suicide.

Months went by as I was soul searching what to do with myself, processing my scars and mental health journey. It was a long undertaking of healing, therapy, journaling, and remembering. I was also interacting with several positive online groups who kept me in the land of the living. They were consistently showing me that I had value to share with the world and supporting my efforts to move forward with the non-profit.

Scars to Stars™ was born.

Our first event was a virtual summit with fifteen speakers, each sharing a vulnerable story about overcoming something in their life. Although we had a small group in attendance, it was an incredible day of supportive and productive conversations. We just passed the two year mark of that event and I have heard from several people that it started the change and healing in their own lives.

Now I understand one hundred percent that what I am doing is making a difference, all without a Psychology degree. Peer to peer support is needed for everyone in their own unique way. For me it was the best support that helped me heal from decades of silence.

"It is not joy that makes us grateful; it is gratitude that makes us joyful."

– David Steindl-Rast

I want to shout out a special thank you to Bari Baumgardner and Sage Events for more than I can say here. In May 2020 I saw a Facebook ad for The Virtual Events on Virtual Events, and I signed up. I did not even know what Zoom was at the time. I had been doing in person events for thirty years; for almost any corporation you can name, but I had no idea what a virtual event would look like.

I figured I did not have anything to lose, maybe I would figure out a way to save my business...

Instead, I met 160 incredible people throughout a year-long program and solidified my new purpose in this world. I made so many new friends and even met a few of them in person! That founding group in the LEAP program was huge in my journey and transformation. Sometimes we just need a new perspective and to surround ourselves with different people.

"Leadership is the responsibility to take care of those around us."

~ Simon Sinek

As a mentor, trainer, manager, executive, speaker, entrepreneur, consultant, and coach, my inclination is always to put others needs before my own. My instinct has always been to help anyone who needs help, or anyone who asks me for help. After so many years in hospitality, I would pick up trash on the sidewalk or say hello to anyone that crossed my path. I felt a duty to help people in need, or to lend a helping hand 'just because'.

I believe that we have a responsibility to our employees or team, to teach and train them to be their best selves. The most impactful leaders are the ones that help the people around them reach their goals. The teams of people who support each other and work together to reach greatness, are the ones that are the most successful.

In addition, as leaders, we must be careful about giving too much of ourselves on a consistent basis. Putting everyone else's needs ahead of our own all the time drains the creativity and drive we need to be successful, so that we can reach the next level. There is no shame in putting yourself first, just like the oxygen on the plane... When we take care of ourselves, it is a sign that we value ourselves, and that we have self-compassion. This comes with time, but it is possible!

My own journey of putting myself last was a focus a couple of years prior to closing my business. The miraculous part of my new self-compassion was that I spent less time working on my business, but the revenue was growing! Thoughtful routines, healthy boundaries, creativity, delegation and implementation made it all possible for me to work less and experience more success.

In my latest book, *The Shower Genius®*, I talk about how self-care breeds creativity, which in turn breeds the ideas and solutions we need to be successful. It is impossible to function at our highest level of productivity when we have brain fog, stress, and overwhelm. If you are sleep deprived and burnt out, who are you really helping?

"The great leaders are not the strongest, they are the ones who are honest about their weaknesses."

~ Simon Sinek

During the pandemic, I started a company called Genius & Sanity. It is a Consulting and Coaching business that focuses on The Shower Genius® Framework, created by yours truly. It is built around my experiences of being an entrepreneur, executive and leader over more than three decades. The main concept is how we can sustain or grow our businesses with our genius, while we simultaneously expand our brain power needed for ideas and solutions that will grow our business without all the stress, exhaustion, and burnout. This all started with a surgery where I was supposed to be out of commission for two weeks; but turned out I was bedridden for two months... and my team did an incredible job while I was away.

After that experience, I started taking steps to take better care of myself. The results were fantastic mentally and physically. They also showed up in business reports as well!

The day I made the decision to get that tattoo on my forearm, I was sitting on a beach in Jamaica with my husband. That trip was supposed to be our fifth anniversary, but it was our sixteenth year of marriage before we got there... I finally learned how to put myself first and grow my business at the same time!

"Growth and Change are continuous processes; not a one and done in ourselves or in business."

~ Deana Brown Mitchell

At The Realize Foundation, our mission is to reduce suicide statistics through conversations, community and personal story. We host all events *(so far)* online so anyone in the world can login and know they are not alone. Our books, Scars to Stars™, are an Amazon bestselling series with stories of vulnerability, resilience and overcoming adversity. Anyone can apply to tell their story in our books, we release them in May for Mental Health Awareness Month and in September for Suicide Prevention Month. We also produce #SaveALifeChallenge Virtual Events each quarter to promote awareness and community.

"Compassion is not a virtue — it is a commitment. It's not something we have or don't have — it's something we choose to practice."

~ Brene Brown

As the title of this chapter states, I am truly *"Thankful for the Scars"* because they have allowed me to broaden my own horizons and help many others do the same. I would not be who I am without them!

Scars Command Acknowledgment *to* Realize Success

Vulnerability, Authenticity and Compassion required!

My hope for you is that this chapter made you FEEL something, and that it will be the catalyst in your own life for the CHANGE you desire and deserve! I pray that you learn to put yourself first before it is too late to enjoy your life, your work, your family, and your dreams!

"I've learned that people will forget what you said,

people will forget what you did,

but people will never forget how you made them feel."

~ Maya Angelou

***

To contact Deana:

www.deanabrownmitchell.com

Subscribe. Find out more about consulting and coaching. Schedule a call. Take the Sanity Quiz!

https://www.linkedin.com/in/deanamitchell/

https://www.facebook.com/deana.b.mitchell/

https://www.instagram.com/geniusandsanity/

Amazon.com: Deana Brown Mitchell: books, biography, latest update

For more information about The Realize Foundation's work:

www.realizefoundation.org

Subscribe. Donate. Register for an Event. Buy our Books. Apply to Tell Your Story!

https://www.linkedin.com/company/the-realize-foundation/

https://www.facebook.com/RealizeFoundation

https://www.instagram.com/realizefoundation/

https://twitter.com/ScarstoStarsTM

https://www.youtube.com/channel/UCr5BgLouFRAcK-15iKFE-uQ

Look for our new podcast, out in summer 2023!

Heather Bach

Heather Bach is an End-of-Life and Grief Doula. By guiding clients in their reflection, prioritization, and planning, Heather helps them clarify what living ãa good life to the very end" looks like to them. She provides emotional, practical, and spiritual support to clients and their loved ones. She works to increase comfort, meaning, and beauty at end-of-life and advocates for clients when they can no longer speak for themselves. She also provides grief support for all kinds of losses and difficult life transitions and guidance for honoring the memory of loved ones who are dearly missed. Heather graduated from the Conscious Dying Instituteäs Sacred Passage Doula and End-of-Life Coach programs. Her education also includes an MA from Georgetown University and a BA from Dartmouth College. Based in La Crosse, WI, Heather is available for in-person and virtual appointments.

Inviting Grief in for Tea

By Heather Bach

I should probably wear a warning label on airplanes or at events where unsuspecting strangers are likely to ask me, ãSo… what do you do for work?" If they started with something like, ãHow many pets do you have?" that would be so much safer. I could tell them about my three cats, two dogs, and my flock of rascally backyard chickens. Or they could ask if I have kids. Yes, one. Heäs a teenager, he's hilarious and smart and I love being his mom. Where am I from? Easy! I was born in Tucson, Arizona. I have also lived in Minnesota, Oregon, New Hampshire, Ecuador, Florida, Virginia, Maryland, and now Wisconsin. Favorite ice cream flavor? Coffee…or dulce de leche…that is a tricky decision, but at least the answer keeps us in territory that doesnät shake up anyoneäs day. But instead of asking strangers what their life is like, we often ask them what they do for a living. Some people arenät ready for my answer. I am an End-of-Life and Grief Doula. My passion is to help people develop a healthier relationship with death and grief. I embrace every opportunity to talk about my work as a Doula, and that means talking about how we, as a society, have forgotten how to die and grieve well. As a result, we are not living as well as we could be. These subjects can make people uncomfortable, but there is usually also some curiosity because most people have never even heard of an End-of-Life Doula.

The word doula comes from the Greek word ãdoulē," which refers to a female attendant or helper. Many people are familiar with birth doulas, who assist before, during, and after the birth of a baby. As an End-of-Life Doula, I serve people in similar ways at the other end of their life journey. I provide a wide variety of non-medical support to people who are dying and to their loved ones after they have died. What this involves varies by client and how far along they are on their journey. Ideally, I will start working with someone long before they qualify for hospice. I hold space for people while they grapple with the news that their diagnosis is terminal. While they still have energy and mobility, we can work on legacy projects and identify their priorities for the time they have left. I facilitate difficult conversations with family. I pick up their favorite treat from a cafe, run errands, take notes during appointments, and advocate for my clients' final wishes when they are too weak to advocate for themselves. Based on what matters most to each client, I ensure their final months, days, and moments are as fulfilling as possible.

I understand why it's difficult for many people to talk about death because I was one of

those people. In fact, I spent most of my life with an unusually high level of fear of both death

and grief. My earliest memories of death were of a complete refusal to accept it as

inevitable or final. When I was four or five years old, I found out that my maternal grandmother

was no longer alive. She had died when I was 9 months old, so I had no memory of her. At some point, I must have had a conversation with my mom about her parents and learned that while she had a dad who was alive, her mom had died. I assume this was the first time anyone had tried to explain death to me. While I don't remember the details of the conversation, I do remember feeling horrified about how hard this had to be for my mom. I loved my mom with all my heart, and I felt I needed her, so I couldn't imagine how my poor mom was surviving without her mom. I came up with the idea that when I grew up, I would figure out how to bring people back from the dead. I imagined inventing something like a seed that you could plant in the ground at a grave, bringing the person back to life. My mom had to explain that her mom had been cremated and had no body to reanimate. The fact that I saw this as only another hurdle to overcome shows the degree to which I was unwilling to accept the concept of death!

I don't remember being especially fearful about my own mortality, but I was terrified of losing people I loved, and I was hurting for my mom. I imagined the pain of having lost her mom to be unbearable. Eventually I grew out of my plan to bring the dead back to life, but other than that, I didn't make a whole lot of progress in my attitude about death over the next 40 years.

Many of my friends lost people they loved as teenagers and young adults. These deaths were hard for me even though, in most cases, I had never even met the person who died. I

suffered on behalf of the people who were left grieving. It seemed so awful to me that they had

to endure these losses. I didnät notice that it was unusual that I suffered so much for these losses

until my freshman year of college when a friend from high school let me know that a mutual

friendäs mom had died. Her response to my grief for this mother I had never met was something

along the lines of äOh Heather, dear…" in a tone of sympathy and pity. I think I noticed then

that our reactions were not the same. She felt sorry for how much she realized I would

suffer rather than being overwhelmed by suffering herself over this mutual friendäs loss.

Even though I realized at that point that I was suffering more than other people over second-hand grief, the only thing I changed was to hide how I felt because I thought I was weird and felt a bit ashamed.

When I was in my 40s, an acquaintance from the local art fair scene, Kathie, posted on Facebook that she had been diagnosed with ovarian cancer. She wrote of her only option being chemotherapy or no chemotherapy. If she chose chemotherapy, it could buy her more time to get her affairs in order. She had approximately two months to live if she decided not to undergo chemotherapy. She never updated her profile regarding her decision, so I didnät know if we were counting down those two months, but I knew that was a possibility. I felt like I should say SOMETHING, but I was so afraid to say the wrong thing that I was paralyzed. Day after day, I said nothing at all.

After several weeks had passed, I finally mustered all my courage and sent her a message. I assumed she had a lot of friends and family that would be rallying to support her, and I was just an acquaintance, but I still wanted to reach out. So, I sent her a message and asked if she needed help with anything. I suggested that perhaps I could give her a ride or pick things up for her. Her response surprised me. She wrote back, asking, ãDo you play Scrabble?" Heck yeah, I play Scrabble! And thatäs how I started going to her house during the brief periods between chemotherapy treatments when she felt up to being social.

The first time I went to her house, I was again terrified of saying the wrong thing. In hindsight, I should have been more afraid of her Scrabble abilities-she was fierce! By overcoming my fears and showing up that first day, I discovered she wasnät surrounded by close friends and family. In fact, she was very lonely. Her husband was battling his own health issues, and her sister lived several hours away. She had a few close friends who lived out of town who would gather when they could to spend time with her. But in general, most people she knew were afraid to show up and confront mortality with her. It was eye-opening for me.

Over the following year, Kathie and I became close friends as she beat all the projections regarding her life expectancy. In the early months, I would show up as early in the morning as I could get there, with a travel mug of coffee in my hand. As soon as I arrived she would open a bottle of white wine. Iäd chug my coffee, and we would go straight to wine and Scrabble. Eventually, she found Scrabble too difficult, and we would just talk. Towards the end, Iäd often sit with her as she drifted in and out of sleep in her hospice bed. We laughed as much as we cried during my visits. I learned that even when we are ãdying," we are still living. Now I wrestle with the word ãdying." We are either living, or we arenät. So where does that leave this word ãdying?"

My time with Kathie also taught me that I COULD do this. I was no longer afraid. I could sit with someone facing their own life coming to an end and bring them comfort. I could support their family. I could positively impact their final months, weeks, and days. I learned never to assume that somebody is surrounded by support and loved ones. I also learned that End-of-Life Doulas exist and that they can play a tremendously important role during a person's final chapter. Ultimately my experiences with Kathie during her last year, and with my father's cancer journey and death, led me to enroll at the Conscious Dying Institute. There I received my training to become an End-of-Life Doula and Coach.

I went into that training program because I wanted to comfort people who were dying, but one of the most important things I learned during my studies and practical training was how bad I was at grieving. I had not even begun to heal from a traumatic death that I had witnessed. I avoided talking about it or thinking about it as much as possible. My therapist didn't even know about it. I also hadn't grieved for my father. I had been so afraid of getting swamped by the sadness and never finding my way out again that I avoided grieving. In the initial weeks after I lost my dad, when I would get hit with a wave of grief, I would go out to my deck and smoke just a little marijuana to numb my feelings. My old behavior from childhood of stubbornly refusing to accept death had evolved into a stubborn refusal to spend time with grief.

Discovering this in myself opened my eyes to the many ways we fail to grieve as a society, especially as we emerge from the pandemic experience where so many people were unable to be with loved ones as they died. People had to figure out how to say good-bye to their dearest family members virtually. No final hugs. No chance to hold their hands. This is coupled with a general lack of skills, knowledge, awareness, and support as to what to do next because we live in a grief-illiterate society. Therapists are essential. Everyone should go to therapy, but grief isn't something we need help with just once a week. Also, if a person doesn't already have a therapist, it can take months to find someone they like and who is available. Friends and family have more flexible availability, but they are often not very good at holding space for people deep in their grief. In their discomfort, and due to their lack of understanding of grief, they ofter have little more to offer than clichés that leave the grief-stricken frustrated rather than comforted. Often, we hold back from turning to friends and family because we don't want to take up their time, or we don't want to make them sad, or we feel like we should be over our grief by now, so we feel ashamed to admit that we still need support even years after experiencing a loss. I can come up with a long list of reasons why I personally didn't turn to my friends and family when I was deep in my grief. Ultimately, I discovered that my struggles with grief made me the perfect person to help others learn to grieve.

I've learned how essential funerals (and rituals in general) are for closure and the grieving process. I learned this during a time when the pandemic prevented many people from attending funerals. Those people's grief journey and healing were getting cut off at the knees. They could not grieve in the company of others. They missed out on the rituals that would bring them a sense of closure that helps us move through the initial stages of grief. In a society where we don't grieve well to begin with, the pandemic made things worse and left a backlog of unresolved grief in the hearts of countless people. This is why an important aspect of my doula practice includes helping people learn how to grieve in healthy ways.

I've learned that people on their end-of-life journey also grieve. They are grieving for the days they will not see, the relationships they will soon leave behind, and the gradual loss of strength and abilities they had previously taken for granted. They grieve for the pain they know their loved ones will feel when they are gone.

I've learned that to grieve is to go on a journey involving the entire range of emotions humans can experience—sadness, anger, regret, guilt, resentment, envy, and fear. In addition, intense love, gratitude, and respect can all make appearances. It is also a physical experience. We feel our grief in our bodies. It can be an ache, an emptiness, fatigue, a loss of appetite, or an urge to cry, scream, or run away. It is also a journey through our thoughts. Following and processing specific thoughts can make grief a transformational process. Grief involves learning who we are after the loss. It often consists of confronting our own mortality. It can inspire a reevaluation of how we live and conduct our relationships.

I've learned that grief is unpredictable. It manifests differently in every individual and with every loss. It is even unpredictable from one moment to the next. A person can be going through their day just fine until some thought or sensory experience reconnects them to their grief in a way that feels like they've just been kicked in the chest. Grief is not depression. It can turn into depression, but they are not the same. It is not something that can be rushed or skipped. When we avoid our grief, it finds ways to catch up with us. If we leave it no other option, it will manifest in our physical and mental health.

Iäve learned that unresolved grief damages relationships, affects our careers, and prevents us from living the full, rich lives we are capable of living. This is why I encourage people to spend time with their grief. I had been so afraid of grief that I was avoiding it. What I needed to do was to invite grief in for some tea and a little conversation. I trust now that when I open the door to grief it won't just march in, take over, and refuse to ever leave. It is not a thug that will overwhelm me physically and somehow smother me. It may feel like too much to befriend it, but I guide people to find ways to improve their relationships with both grief and death. With another person at the table with you, sharing a pot of tea with grief feels safer. The conversation may be uncomfortable, but we are not meant to be always comfortable. In fact, uncomfortable conversations are essential to all relationships, including our relationship with grief. I encourage people to find where grief resides in their bodies and pay attention to those places. I remind them to listen to what grief asks them to feel and think about and acknowledge these things.

For me, the two greatest honors of my life have been motherhood and the opportunity to accompany people on their end-of-life and grief journeys. Through my work with clients and conversations with strangers, I hope to inspire a shift in attitude. I want to encourage people to think and discuss how they want their life to end and what scares them about mortality. I want to normalize talking about and honoring losses of all kinds: lost family members, lost pets, lost limbs, lost opportunities, and global losses from events like humanitarian crises, climate change, and environmental disasters. I want employers to recognize the importance of supporting grieving employees and to recognize that many kinds of loss result in grief. It doesnät matter what the loss is. What matters is how significant the impact is on the person who is grieving. If a loss feels devastating, it deserves to be recognized as devastating by the broader community of friends, family, and employers. As a society, we will thrive when all kinds of grief are honored by those experiencing the loss and those around them. This is a big project. I hope you will join me in this by spending some time thinking about how grief has impacted your life and paying attention to ways in which you perhaps have not allowed yourself to grieve. You can start by heating a pot of water for tea.

***

To contact Heather:

Voice or text: 507-312-4356

heather@heatherbach.com

www.heatherbach.com

Susan Kennard

Susan Kennard is known as a Spiritual Scientist, a specialist in Early Childhood Trauma. Susan was originally a Psychologist and Psychotherapist working in the field of Child Protection. She has over 20 years of extensive experience working with trauma including Veterans and PTSD. Susan works mostly on Zoom allowing distance to be no barrier. Susan is a published author and her work "Awaken the Light Within Your Heart: A Guide to Self-Healing" has helped many to heal and step onto their spiritual path to create lasting success in their lives. Susan has appeared on national TV, Newspapers and magazines and is regularly interviewed about her innovative and transformative work and teaching on international tele-summits, podcasts and other media platforms. Susan is a professional speaker and presenter and speaks publicly about her research and new innovations within her work. Susan hosts her own Podcast, The Spiritual Awakener and to reach those ready to align with their mission. Susan's work helps you to release fear, allowing LOVE and more light to be reflected from your cells into your inner and outer experience. Your external life is a mirror, and it is this mirror that tells you how you are vibrating. By combining her traditional training and her spiritual gifts, Susan helps you to remember that you are your own inner healer and that you can create a free and abundant life by aligning to your true mission.

Our Journey to Awakening the Light Within our Hearts.

By Susan Kennard

Our soul knew before we came what we were supposed contribute to this life. If you are reading this then I am sure you are someone that has awakened to the remembering of who you are a divine spark of light just wearing a jacket to hold your soul whilst you carry out your divine mission here on Earth.

Sometimes, however you may dip in and out of the remembering. Sometimes you put one foot back into the old earth, the fear, guilt and lack perceptions can then pop in. Our soul and our higher guidance is always firmly in the present of the new golden earth we are creating. This earth is filled with expansion. This also includes those who push our buttons and can temporarily cause us to doubt our power and sovereignty.

Remembering who you are is the most important piece of the puzzle. If you can imagine we are all born knowing that we have an abundance inheritance that we can tap into at any time, a bit like a spiritual bank account.

When we step into remembering who we are; a soul having a human experience and that we came for a special reason to be of service in our unique way then we know we are not on our own.

If we believe that we are alone and we are doing this journey of life alone, then it can be difficult for us to turn on the tap of abundance. This abundance stream is not just a monetary currency; it is a person-to-person currency too. This can be the souls who seem to show up at the perfect time, the books you feel guided to read, the words that someone speaks to you in a café, all are examples of abundance.

As we are awakening our light within our heart, we realise that we are so much more than our physical body or mind. We remember that we are an integrated being, a co-creator with the universe and we truly can choose and create anything we desire.

A problem of lack can show up in our lives when we have perceptions of belief that put blocks in the way of what we desire. This is a bit like dust on a mirror. You can still see though that mirror but by polishing it, the reflection becomes clearer and brighter. This is exactly how it is when you do the inner work and heal childhood beliefs. As your mirror becomes brighter, the reflection of abundance comes to you more easily and freely. With no blame and definitely no shame, is it time to clean your mirror?

The information below is taken from my book Awaken The Light Within Your Heart, a guide to self-healing. Enjoy the excerpts I have chosen to share with you, which include a combination of channelled healing from the guides, my inner child processes and a little bit about me.

In June 2021 I was blessed to be one of the winners of the Hay House Writers' competition. I put my heart and especially my soul into the energy of my book and with the help of my spirit teams, I set the intention that it would reach the many so that we all could remember who we are, that we can heal and that we are free to choose the path our soul chose.

Published by Balboa Press, Hay House- October 2022. You can purchase my book in all formats including audio at amazon worldwide.

<u>Awaken The Light Within Your Heart by Susan Kennard</u>

We are in the midst of massive global change. And while so many unknowns lie ahead for humanity, it's clear we all have an opportunity to heal and step fully into the life we came to lead. In fact, it's necessary for us to do this inner work so that we can create the monumental change this world is craving and needing. Awaken the Light Within helps readers do this with ease. This book is written for those who want to understand themselves more deeply and to heal on a profound level. It teaches the reader to remember who each of us is: a soul choosing to have a human experience. It guides the reader to align to their divine mission and in doing so to live an abundant life with harmonious relationships. The profound yet easy-to-follow process outlined in this book guides readers in releasing blocks from the past—whether these may be from childhood, past life imprints, or their ancestral lines—and awaken the light within their own hearts. Once ignited, this light allows us to step forward to fully align with our mission, activate the intuitive inner guidance we need, and become the people we were meant to be—the people this world needs during this transformational time. When we are held energetically captive by the past, our potential is severely limited, and we are often prevented from living in freedom, which is our sovereign birth right. We often struggle in our health, our relationships, our access to resources, and much more. Our perceptions and limiting beliefs lead us to choose mediocre lives and experiences, accept less than our true worth, and muffle the voice of our inner guidance. We struggle to see clearly the path meant for us and end up stuck in dead-end and unfulfilling situations that keep us from shining our essential light into the world and being of service in our chosen mission here.

What makes Awaken the Light Within unique and important is that it integrates the latest knowledge about trauma healing with a clear step-by-step process that readers can do on their own for profound and lasting transformation. The book weaves in healing codes and channelling from my team of guides, adding potency and support for readers' experiences by elevating their vibration. It also includes numerous success stories in the form of testimonials from people who have experienced tremendous benefit in utilizing these light-awakening processes.

A little about my spiritual awakening

At 27 years old, I was awoken in the early hours of morning by a telephone call. It was a girl telling me that a dear friend of mine, a previous boyfriend, had taken his life. Lots of emotions and thoughts arose. Maybe I could have helped. Why didn't he let me know? And the big question: why?

This was a man who appeared to have it all. On paper, he did. His parents were wealthy, he wanted for nothing, and he had his own pizza franchise. But previously I remembered that he had told me that his girlfriend had become pregnant and that he had made her have an abortion. I think that was one of the reasons he left—he couldn't cope with the guilt and regretted it. I was devastated. Martin had been so important in my life that I later chose to name my son after him to keep his memory alive. He had been living in his home country of New Zealand, and because it was on the other side of the world, I couldn't go to the funeral. At the time, I was finishing my postgraduate degree in psychotherapy and living in London, working as a nanny for two young children. The parents worked for BBC radio and were amazingly supportive. Then it happened: I had been getting on with my life, when one night, a few months after I had received the news about Martin, I was woken again, this time by a feeling that someone was in the room. I sensed the presence of someone, and a dog too. I was asleep and yet awake. I couldn't move. I could see but not through my eyes—with an inner vision. I felt someone touch my shoulder gently, shaking me as if to wake me up. I admit I was scared in that moment, as I had never experienced anything like that. It was surreal yet profound. As quickly as it had come, it was gone. I did not know at this point that it was Martin and his sausage dog, who had passed six months before he had.....

A note from the guides on healing

Our ability to heal ourselves is infinite. We have the power to selfheal, so why do we feel we have to hand our power over to another to heal us? Granted, we definitely need the medical model; the universe has given this way of healing so that in certain circumstances, such as accidents and operations, we can utilise it. However, if we were able to remember that we can heal ourselves, would we visit our doctor as much as we perhaps have in the past? Here is how my guides responded to these questions.

Guides: We want you to remember that you were born with the knowledge that you have infinite power and that you can heal any part of your energy field at any time. We channel this information for you at this time, as we have noticed that fear has over taken many on your planet, and indeed in your society. We want to offer you a simple way to access and heal yourself. Essentially, we would like you to gain back your power and be more fully in alignment with unconditional love. We are those speaking as the council of light, and we work on a high-vibrational frequency toning through this loving channel of light named Susan. We do this to raise the frequency in your heart field, allowing you the ability to reflect light more readily within your cells. With this brighter reflection, your life reflects back to you in that same high-vibrational light. So essentially your life becomes lighter, your body becomes free, and you are attracted to the pure and abundant opportunities that flood in. You always knew this, as it was part of your purpose to remember who you are. Those who are reading or listening this are ready to embark on the journey of self-healing. If you can imagine that you are just a light, then as we look at you, we can see any interruptions in your field. We see these interruptions clearly, as does the channel writing this information for you. When you can access the interruptions in your own light field and heal them, you are free. With this new-found freedom, you are fully able to be a bringer of your light. We love you and wish to assist you on your healing journey. We know that many of you are experiencing great fear in the realms of your planet. We wish you to know that in a moment of realisation, this fear is not real, and the illusion of what you are seeing disappears. So you may ask, why do we feel fear if it's not real? You feel fear because it is part of your emotional body to experience many emotions. You chose to send the feeling to the universe to expand not only your consciousness but the universe exponentially. You chose to allow emotions to flow through your heart, not to inhibit you. This is your learning and expansion. We are so grateful that you chose to volunteer to be here at this time, to bring your light and raise the vibration of the planet. It was all an experiment—nothing more, nothing less. This does not take away, however, from your experience; just as you came to experience fear, you came to experience unconditional love of yourself. This, we see, you find the hardest task in the human form you chose. We smile as the channel is writing this, as we know that you were so excited to experience all these emotions and see how they affected your physical form. However, now you are present in human form, it is not such an exciting experience. We smile with love and gratitude for the journey you have chosen. It is for us too, and we stand fully by your side at all times.

A powerful healing process from my book- Cutting the ties that bind with forgiveness

This process has shown to clear old contracts, past lives, instantly heal marriages, help divorce or heal without needing divorce, heal mother or father relationships or relationships with bosses, work colleagues, and even abusers. You can even cut the ties with those who have passed over to spirit.

We are all connected, and the relationships that show up outside of us that trouble us are actually a mirror of our own frequency. This can be lack of self-love, anger resentment, fear, loss—whatever emotion shows up in the other is in part a reflection of us.

When we heal these unwanted emotions, our vibration can hold more light, and therefore we reflect the vibration of more love out to the world and the world shows it back. This is shown in our relationships too.

Enjoy the process:

- Imagine a person here or in spirit with whom you would like to heal your relationship. Remember, this is just to cut the ties that bind, that don't serve you, not the loving bonds or marriages in this life—unless of course they are no longer for your highest and best good.
- Ground yourself, place your hands on your heart, breathe and then imagine your Earth Star under your feet and your*Soul Star above your head. Imagine the person that you wish to cut the emotional ties with to join you in your mind. You are connecting with their soul, and they know that this will help them too, so don't worry about asking them—it's not needed.
- As you look at them and they look at you, how do you feel? What emotions come up for you?
- It's not your job to heal them, so we will do that for you. Imagine in front of them a beam of pure light. Imagine them stepping into this light and receiving pure connection to Source, unconditional love, and whatever else they need. If you prefer, just hand it over and know that they will receive exactly what they need to heal.
- Notice now how you feel when you look at them.
- Has something changed for you?
- Next it's time to cut the ties that have bound to you lifetime after lifetime, stopping you from being free.
- Say to them, "Today from a place of unconditional love, I choose to set myself free, and as I do this, I set you free

too. I choose to forgive myself as I choose to forgive you. I let go of anything from any lifetime, past, present or future that does not serve us. I choose to release any pacts, agreements, vows, oaths, marriages, religious orders, blood bindings, chains, sacrifices, written and verbal contracts, and any lifetimes of slavery or feeling trapped in any way, in any timeline or lifetime. I do this with unconditional love deep within my soul."

- Check in with how you feel now. What has changed?
- Then say their name and "I feel "— whatever you want to say that you haven't been able to say.
- Really speak from the heart. For example: "I feel that you have made me wrong, betrayed me, hurt me."
- From a place of unconditional love, say, "I am setting us free."
- Watch them float off, or you can bring them into your heart.
- If it is a current relationship, you can always ask the true soul reason for why you are together, the mission you have.
- Focus on your heart, take time for you and breathe and when you are ready you can open your eyes and come back to the present.

Closing words from the guides

You chose to inhabit a physical form and in that moment you knew who you were, you remembered your essence. When you placed the jacket of your body around you, you chose to forget. You chose to forget initially so that you could listen to your soul and follow your mission. With your physical body jacket on, and your emotions flowing, remember that you are connected to everything and everyone. This is an expression of love itself. You chose to experience free will, to choose, to create and to manifest by remembering love itself. Live your life with joy in your heart, nothing more nothing less.

Do you need more?

If you have enjoyed reading these excerpts from my book Awaken the Light Within, I would invite you to consider the next steps on your mission. I offer many ways for the guides and I to help you. Visit my website to learn about my Souls Mission Membership and to attend my monthly healing retreats. Take a look at www.susankennard.co.uk

It's my intention that in your lifetime you will align fully to your soul's mission and help to co-create the new golden abundant earth that is for humanity to enjoy.

***

To contact Susan:

Website: www.susankennard.co.uk

Email: susan@susankennard.co.uk

Youtube: https://www.youtube.com/@SusanKennard/videos

Facebook: https://www.facebook.com/SusanKSparkleToSuccess

Facebook: https://www.facebook.com/susan.kennard.58/

Instagram: https://www.instagram.com/susankennard1/

Linkedin: https://www.linkedin.com/in/susan-kennard-78b10435/

TikiTok: tiktok.com/@susankennard1

Rose Marie Young

Rose Marie Young resigns in the beautiful province of Ontario Canada. She is the Co-Founder and Executive Director of The BloomGlow Foundation. She is the visionary creator of PASSION Self-Empowerment Business Supporting Business Magazine. She is also an Empowerment Life Coach, who is inspired and committed to helping her clientele overcome post-traumatic experiences so they can live the life they desire without feeling guilty. Rose Marie is the visionary compiler of two International Best-Selling Anthologies, including her latest Anthology, The Rising Eagles. She also co-authored Pursued by Passion, and in Volume 5 book of You Can Overcome Anything. Her true expression of life can be found in her zestfulness for writing inspirational articles and poems. Some of Rose's articles have been featured live in Thrive Global Publications and other publications such, as Successful-hack.com and others.

Rose worked as a certified Cardiologist Technologist prior to becoming an Empowerment Trauma Life Coach. She also studied Industrial Microbiology and Medical Laboratory Technology as well. Rose loved and appreciated working in the medical field. However, Rose Marie has found great fulfillment in nature, coaching, and in helping others to improve themselves. While she herself is constantly and intentionally thriving for inner growth.

Contagious Energy

By Rose M Young

It was an incredibly long journey back to a place where I was able to find my truth, where I was able to identify my purpose and became aware of who I was. I was broken, lost, and totally unaware of what was happening. My energy was extremely low, and I had lost almost everything to the darker side of sadness, guilt, and frustration. Everyone around me was feeding off the same navigating negative energy as well. It was contagious. My fire was totally burnt out. The spark I had all along was gone. It was a big change, by far the biggest challenge of my life, as my entire life was turned upside down. I had two choices, to give up or to keep pushing.

I remembered it well; it was a magnificent, beautiful day, April 4th, 2008, to be exact. I was in the cardiac office wishing for the shift to be over so I could go outside and enjoy the luminous sunshine before it when down. I was happy when I finally finished with the last patient; I was able to leave. I believe the universe was trying to tell me something that day because not long after I started the journey home, I began to encounter an unusual amount of evening traffic. The rush hour had started, and I kept thinking I should take a different route. I ignored the thoughts and continued along the main road. That was not a good idea. Within five to ten minutes of driving, I came to a set of lights. I stopped just as the light turned red. Red... That means stop, right? Well, one person driving a very gigantic vehicle, two other cars behind didn't think so. I assumed the driver was going to stop, but he did not. From the rear view of my car, I could see what was about to happen. It was going to be big; it was going to be major!!

Looking up through the rear-view mirrors, I embraced myself for the sudden impact. Bang! And, another Bang, and a very loud crash.

The sound forever printed in my brain was a sound I will never forget. As I closed my eyes and held tightly to the wheel of the car, I heard that loud noise of the impact, then all the lights went out. At that moment, my entire life flashed before me. I remembered keeping my eyes closed for quite a while as the car I was driving was hit from behind. Then I slowly opened my eyes and although in shock, I was more than happy to be alive.

At first, I thought I was dreaming, but realized that I was not when the street became paved with almost every emergency personnel in the immediate area. Police, ambulances, tow trucks, fire trucks, and all. Although I and the others involved were injured, we were very lucky no one died that day.

I remember being in the ambulance to the hospital, thinking of the twisted metals of my car. The teardrops flooded my face until my eyes hurt. I felt the pain as it rushed through my entire body that day, but I wasn't prepared for the painful aches, emotional ups and downs, sleepless nights, and other complications and challenges that were awaiting me.

The pain was unbelievable, unbearable. At one point I was told to get rid of the pain in my back and left leg, I need to have back surgery. I did not instead, I pumped at least 10 different pills into my body each day to help with the pain as well as with other issues that occurred due to the accident. My stomach and my inner organs hated me for doing so. I was beyond stressed. I had problems getting it together. I certainly did not know how to cope. After a short while, I ended up losing a job I had worked in for years. To make matters worse, my friends started to disappear one after the other. I was no longer on their list of people to hang out with. I was very sad and heartbroken. I was also no longer the fun mom my children knew. I was lost within myself and became a prisoner of the cold darkness of my bedroom with the curtains drawn. It was my safest place, my getaway from the world place. After a few years, I decided to drive again, but to my disappointment, I was in another four-car multi-vehicle accident, yet again It would be about six years before I was able to get back to work. I anticipated that day because I knew nothing was going to be the same.

I was determined to get my life back in order. I was physically, financially, and emotionally stressed. I was drowning in a flood of negative emotions. I was becoming a person that I truly did not know nor even care to know. Each day was becoming more and more stressful. I needed a sense of purpose and some motivation. Besides all odds and tormented by pain and sleepless nights of mares, I got a glimpse of hope when I first started to write to the universe "Thank You" notes and made promises of all the things I would do for repayment of getting better. At that time, there were so many different unfamiliar voices in my head, voices of discouragement, isolation, doubt, fears, and anxiety; I had voices telling me to give up. What choice did I have? I thought to myself, "what If I did give up, who would even care? What response did I have to keep moving forward? Then after melting down for what seemed like a lifetime, I was drained, but I suddenly snapped out of the pity for myself. I found a reason and a purpose for wanting to fight for recovery, to fight for the mystery of life that lies ahead. I found a reason to keep it together, my Children.

What is your reason for pushing forward?

Each day lived, we are born again, and with each new day, our energy source is recharged. Through our vibrational energy, positive or negative, it is harnessed within and transformed outward by our thoughts and actions. Our expression creates the illusion of our existence and the changes we experience. Knowing that energy is transferable and highly contagious, we should become more aware of everything we do, and even how we choose to deal with the challenges we are given in life. We should always keep in mind that everything we do will influence the lives of others. We should be extremely careful in our coping mechanisms as well. Excessive drinking, eating, or even trying to figure things out by us is never the answer. We are tested with changes that happen in our life, and if we do not pass these tests, they will be repeated over and over until the lesson for each specific test has been learned. Life is a constant push, to elevate, grow, and be better than our best.

As individuals, each of us is the only one with the power to change our own thinking patterns. We are the decision-makers and action-takers of our own thoughts. We can create the vibrational energy we desire. It is true, the universe is always giving to us what we are consciously or unconsciously focused on. Every day is an opportunity and a chance to create our own perspective on life and how we fit in. Regardless of our great expectations, things, people and environmental factors such as the atmosphere can become major influences on our actions. There is always going to be a battle between one's individual mind and his or her will to survive. Our survival is based on our concept of changes and how we embrace and grow from them. Despite the hurdles, we must overcome the battles we face. We can change for the better. I recall one of my favorite childhood rhymes that goes, "Good, better, best; never let it rest until your good is better, and your better best." I never fully understood what it all meant until I was grown. How we relate to our past experiences, our mindsets, and what lessons we gained is rather very important to the choices we make.

I believe our life experiences are our legacies, our true teachers, and the main fundamentals of our stories. Each story is unique to each specific person. Some may choose to engage in sharing their own experiences while others may continue to carry it within themselves and eventually, get buried with it, 'taking it to the grave'".

One needs to be intentionally and mentally focused on their recovery if they need healing or be consciously aware of their actions regardless of their situation all attention should be on a positive outcome and not focus on any negative distractions that are toxic to one's overall. wellbeing When we are faced with challenges, our mind automatically goes into a "what if" mode. Sometimes people tend to think of the negative sides of things before even thinking of all the amazing things that can have a great result attached. To overcome each change and each challenge, I had to focus on one thing, the feeling of being well, As the saying goes, "if it doesn't serve you, pick a new thought that does. Everything begins with a thought. My belief is to think from the end but be intentionally present in the moment. However, we can develop a habit of creating our moments as they please us. Keep in mind that your story now is another person's roadmap to help them navigate through the jungle of life. Your story will help them find their own way to a much better in their life. Your story is an empowerment toolbox that others will need to enhance them, to motivate and encourage them to embrace their own.

Do not despise small steps or small beginnings, because each small step we take will eventually take us to our desired destinations. Embrace life as it unfolds and try your best to enjoy it. Always give thanks for little achievements. Keep in mind that something big does not have to always happen or show up for it to be impactful. Energy is contagious, so always be in the company of other people with positive energy. Trust in your journey and your progress. It can be as simple as one very small step. It is okay to set goals, but once you have achieved those goals, keep moving forward. Setting goals can be very good; however, if you're not aware, goals can also limit your growth. If you believe you can, it is ok to set unlimited goals. "Don't reach for the stars, reach beyond the stars". Sometimes, we cannot see beyond the limits of the goals we set for ourselves, but changes, sometimes unexpectedly challenge us to see surpass those limits. never understate your greatness.

Trying to accept the responsibility for someone else's happiness is never your job. Despite the situation, it is okay to create your own happiness. Do what makes you happy without feeling guilty about it. I used to think that if I was not happy, I was making everyone around me unhappy. I now believe it not to be true. Instead, what I have proven to be true is that whatever I was feeling on the inside, was also attractive on the outside. My outside world mirrors my inner world. Everything in our life starts from inside, therefore, knowing that to be so, our own happiness also must come from within. Never try to complicate your own life with things that are beyond your control. Always keep your life simple and embrace and enjoy the beautiful creation of nature. Always give thanks and show appreciation for each day.

As mentioned, it is a good thing to keep your life simple because a complicated life and lifestyle without direction can be bondage for a person as much as a broken past that had been left unresolved. I believe that almost everyone can agree that living a happy and healthy life should not have any complications attached to it. However, sometimes it does. Unexpected change can sometimes force us to act and react in ways that we would rather not. Like an onion, as life unfolds, we are challenged to grow and learn. Some of these growing experiences may even

leave scars of reminder. I see our scars, visible or invisible, as badges of honor, and each one that the universe presents us is for us to use as an inspirational affirmation, and to help us move forward into our

Devine purpose. The choice is always up to us to decide what we want.

I believe that it is fair to say that we live a predictable, as well as a contagious life based on the affirmation of what we send out to others, to ourselves, and to the universe. Both our energy and our words are affirmations of what we want. Constantly we are thinking, speaking, writing, and taking action. Consciously and unconsciously, we are implementing this application as affirmations to create our daily life. All our words and thoughts are openly spoken or not with or without action will create action. Changes in and around us are the result of all our actions. We sometimes blame others for what is happening in our lives and at times even what is happening in the world, but we all play a part when the dots are connected. Keep in mind that even though it is an initial or an introduction to cause an action. So be aware of what you are thinking of. It is true, "life is exactly what you make it". So, make it a good one. Change can be testing, but it is very necessary. Change causes changes in and around us, and I believe that is a good thing. For without changes, nothing would exist. You and I would not be.

Changes can be a combination of several factors such as physical, spiritual, biological environmental, and others. Each of which is a direct result of something that we did or did not do. Keep in mind that not taking any action is also considered as acting, which means that we are part of this vast universe, and we are all connected even if we believe did not generate any of the changes. Do not get derailed from yourself, when changes happen in life. Remember, life is a voyage, and you get to choose your own destination. If any obstacle hinders you, you also have the choice to take another route or if possible, remove that obstacle. Use the experience of others to guide you or learn from the lessons of your own life experiences, if you yourself have been down that path before. Ask for help if you need it, but do not get stuck.

I know from my own personal experiences, there is a very high level of discomfort with any shift or changes; as for me, I was not always cozy with changes that challenged me in my quest to find myself, but I learned that how I cope with the challenges was more important than what I felt about the challenges. I did not enjoy them, nor did I like them, but I learned to embrace them and even challenged myself to overcome each of them one by one. It was the ultimate battle of empowerment, the battles of self-discovery and self-acceptance, and taking full responsibility, as well as forgiveness. It was an incredible journey, but it was an expedition that was required.

Sometimes our worst days or our worst moments can motivate us and can lead us to our greatest successes in life. Your dark times can often lead to the highlight of life,

Over the years I have been faced with many challenges, but I have learned from each one of them. I called these hurdles. "Life Triggers" Not only do they trigger me to keep moving forward, but they trigger me to stay awake and to remain conscious of what is going on in and around me. They also help me to focus on my actions and how I choose to respond.

It comes down to our commitment and our drive to accept change. Changes challenge us to find solutions. If one solution does not work, and you are not happy, try another. The key is to keep trying until you are happy with a solution that works for you. Never give up. One of my many sayings is "Never leave yourself behind" Be committed to being uncomfortable now, so you be

comfortable later. Every day is a fresh start. Just do not stay stuck in an uncomfortable position forever. Remember that changes and challenges that we sometimes describe as problems can create endurance. Do not be afraid to take chances that will help you in your quest for betterment and life abundance. Sometimes the things that we are most afraid of are the things that are holding us back. I have had many things that were holding me back before, However, I decided to challenge myself and pressed the reset bottom. Today, I am living each day intentionally. Life is not always perfect, but even when things seem dark, there can be positivity and light in the world by adjusting our attitude toward the darkness in any situation. If the focus is on the light (Positive Vibrations), the universe will give us more of the same when we are faced with the darker side of things.

Pain in any area of life shows that there is a need for change. To make a change, or to embrace change, is a process that is needed for our creator to use us to fulfill our true purpose and reason for our exitance.

***

To Contact Rose:

Website:www.Rosemarieyoung.com

Facebook: Rose Young902

Instagram: Rose.Marie. young

Email: rosemarie.lifecoach@gmail.com

Email:rmarie1695@gmail.com

Dr. Tianna Conte

Dr. Tianna Conte is a unique blend of trailblazing mystic, eternal entrepreneur and researcher of human consciousness. She is the founder of the Awakening Awareness Academy that empowers visionary entrepreneurs, transformational leaders and healing experts to escape from the hamster wheel of stress and financial struggle. This freedom is so as to live successfully and fulfilled in actualizing their soul's calling in service of others.

Imagine navigating life's challenges by re-awakening your divine guidance and soul's superpowers. The result is experiencing true freedom, authentic intimacy, and love that never dies starting with yourself.

Her signature program, The GPS Code™ (God/Source Positioning System) directs your soul through an ego-friendly spiritual system that specializes in r-evolutionary self-care and personal transformation.

After spiritual awakenings, including a near-death-experience, Tianna brings an intuitive knowing for accelerating your entrepreneurial journey. Her career has spanned 45 years as a naturopath, interfaith minister, initiated shaman, Reiki master and psycho-spiritual therapist specializing in mind/body energy medicine.

Tianna is an international best-selling author of multiple books on self-transformation, including her true-life spiritual romance: Love's Fire: Beyond Mortal Boundaries and Love's Fire: Living the Awakened Journey. She also co-stars in documentaries with enlightened luminaries such as Rev Michael Beckwith and T. Harv Eker.

Tianna has traveled to over 55 countries around the globe working with shamans, spiritual masters and personal development experts to further evolutionary exploration into self-actualization. Her expertise focuses on training others to live life with passion, purpose, prosperity and pleasure.

Extraordinary Journey

By Dr. Tianna Conte and Rev. Azima Jackson

"Those who are awake live in a state of constant amazement." -
Buddha

What do the words "extraordinary journey," mean to you? What images or wisdom come to mind? Are you enjoying and relating to your life as extraordinary? For us, the word "extra" stands out and becomes extra--ordinary.

What we know to be true is for an extraordinary journey, there needs to be something extra. What do you believe goes into the extra? For us, the extra is living beyond the five senses. This is living as if the mind was a sixth sense, as noted by quantum physicist Fred Alan Wolf in the movie we produced, <u>Awaken Your Riches</u>. This awareness was exemplified supernaturally by Tianna's NDE (Near Death Experience) and Azima's mortal encounter with death. The polarity of these experiences became the foundation of the messages and principles that Tianna and Azima are here to share. The essence is in accessing the guidance and invisible power available to all of us.

Everything is perception. Our perception can keep us small or beckon us to evolve. Everything is energy, as proven by quantum physics. Many have heard "glass half empty, glass half full." Einstein states it best, "There are two ways to live: You can live as if nothing is a miracle; you can live as if everything is a miracle."

Are you aware of the magnificence of who you are? To perceive oneself through mere mortal eyes of the body limited by skin boundaries and brain limited by thoughts and beliefs taken from pre-birth to age eight would be a travesty. Intuitively, as children, we all engage in the magic of possibilities. Unfortunately, for many, this is conditioned out through well-meaning parents and authorities who want to raise us to the ways of the world. They project their limitations on us as if they are the experts. The biggest fallacy is now continued.

We are here to erase the limitations placed on us and take back our divine destiny, as stated best in the words of the French philosopher Pierre Teilhard de Chardin, "We are not human beings having a spiritual experience. We are spiritual beings having a human experience."

We are bigger than we appear to be. We are talking about beings of frequency beyond what we can experience through the five senses. Tianna intuitively knew this; her near-death experience (NDE) in 1995 proved it to her. Without getting into the details, her NDE was not through accident or disease. It was through a body wrap meant to destress. This story can be found in <u>Love's Fire: Beyond Mortal Boundaries</u>. The following words, and an invitation to a life review, forever changed Tianna's perception. Her life was enhanced indelibly. Our desire is to enhance your life, as well, without the need for an NDE.

"Birth and death are the same. One is celebrated, and one is feared. One is celebrated because it is known; one is feared because it is unknown...but both are about essence. One is essence taking on form, and the other is essence leaving form behind, returning to Oneness. But both are the same.

The period of time between what is birth and what is death is called life. It is about experiences, experiencing many things, unfolding the truth of one's nature, of expanding awareness of who you really are and the gifts you bring...discovering that love is a frequency, not an emotion. Only love is real. All else is appearance, a part of the illusion created by the senses, and the illusion of separation. Each person is in physical form to give and receive love and so therefore expanding the truth of one's being.

Soon after the above words, what proceeded to unfold was a review of my life. It started from pre-birth and spanned the years to my present age. It came in the form of movie vignettes. I experienced each event of agony— not necessarily agonizing pain, but a painful memory. I experienced what I had felt, what I had thought about it, the choices and decisions that I had made—all of it. However, this is where they had an uncanny twist. I witnessed the memories with no judgment, as if I were watching the unfoldment of a perfect script.

As if by divine magic, light penetrated these memories, almost dissolving them. This light uncovered a picture far greater than my mind could have fathomed. Somehow the light of that presence shone through to reveal that each occurrence held within it a gift that was greater than the pain of the experience. As such, these memories of agony could be viewed as growing pains. Indeed everything, bar none, served...regardless of my own judgments...Every one of my experiences had a purpose in some divine design....I feel confident in saying that those moments that cause the greatest pain can also contain the seeds of our spiritual awakening."

As a therapist and shaman, Tianna realized that as we go over and over the pain of our life story, we solidify its limiting beliefs rather than releasing them and triumphantly transforming them. We need to experience the pain fully and release it as soon as we can. Her quest became the desire to pass the gift of a life review on to others without liability. Not knowing or getting logically caught up in the "how to," she trusted that all would be revealed. Eventually, she met a doctor whose audio CDs effortlessly addressed the issues. This became the first piece of the puzzle.

Together they designed a journey that is a cross between a vision quest and a life review, empowering people to shift to a foundation based on life-enhancing beliefs. Since each person is unique in their memories and experiences, the work is customized. It takes them from pre--birth through the birthing experience, childhood, culminating in Maslow's hierarchy of basic needs fulfilled in the present.

As the universe would have it, the gifts of the NDE continued to manifest and pass on to others in ever-expanding ways. Clearly ensconced in the knowing that all is frequency, and we are that, a friend introduced Tianna and Azima to a computerized energy-based machine.

This energy machine uses modern technology and an ancient prayer modality known as the Tibetan prayer wheel to access the benefits of a higher frequency and divine possibilities. This tool takes one's intentions, releases subtle energy blocks, and sends blessings and prayers for transformation. This technology works with a full-length photo of the person requesting balance. It bathes your picture with vibrations that first clear and then balance your energy field as it subtly reduces stress.

As we were writing this, Tianna realized that the energy machine is the closest to duplicating, on autopilot, an invisible power to dissolve the blocks that blind one's perception of the divine blueprint, similar to her NDE.

Tianna's "aha" moments continued as she realized another piece of her NDE puzzle had unfolded. She had recalled that during her NDE, she was bathed in a Light and frequency of Love that was beyond words and "the peace of God which passes all understanding" (John, Bible). Upon hearing this, Azima was inspired to mention the quote from 1 John in the Bible, "God is love."

At this point, Tianna played with the words she heard in the NDE. "Love is a frequency, not an emotion." For the first time, she expanded it to say, "God is a frequency, not a religion... God is Love". This awareness rang true for both of them, and they were humbled by its message.

The famous quote of Rumi came alive,

> "I belong to no religion.
>
> My religion is Love.
>
> Every heart is my temple."

To our amazement, as we continued to craft this chapter, we witnessed the most significant piece of the NDE puzzle come into visibility. Despite her hesitancy, Tianna felt pressed to express the memories of the trauma and tragedy that happened when she was thirteen years old. The essence, without the details, is that Tianna's father (her hero, doctor/mentor) died, and she was sexually violated the same day by a trusted relative. We both recognized that this sacred wound was crying out to deliver the ultimate message that Tianna had heard energetically and never understood ("In time, Truth will be revealed.").

Although the young Tianna had raged in agony at the force called God during her darkest hours, she had been embraced by an energy of Love that filled her with an ecstasy of Light. It was similar to that experienced in her NDE decades later. For the first time, she had also heard the voice of guidance as a loving power that she affectionately related to intimately as God. The first words were:

> Surrender
>
> Each day
>
> Step by step
>
> You will be shown the way" (Love's Fire: Living the Awakened
>
> Journey)

Speaking and listening to this voice became a daily discipline and undergirding to transforming Tianna's life from tragedy to triumph! Accessing this awareness became the foundation of a life's calling that spanned forty years of empowering others through her gifts. Her longing had always been to free people from self--imposed limitations and dependency on outside guidance.

This force had mystically aligned Tianna to perceive and live life from the inside out. She realized that most people were conditioned to live life from the outside in. Her burning desire became, "How could this wisdom and transformational shift be passed on?" The humorous answer to her prayer was through the bite of a poisonous brown recluse spider on our land in Costa Rica.

As Tianna's healing journey progressed with a combination of minimal medical intervention coupled with innate wisdom, a system emerged. Each day, a vision appeared as she peered and applied the cream and gauzed the deep holes in her toes created by the spider's poison eating to the bone. One step, each day for five days, followed by five more days of hand signals and gestures, and a seeming miracle unfolded. Not only were Tianna's toes made whole, but so was the code made manifest for others to take their steps with a simple blueprint for guidance and power. The same words Tianna heard at thirteen could be duplicated for all!

We are honored to introduce this system, affectionately called the GPS Code. The acronym, GPS, is **God-Source Positioning System** for those who are comfortable with God as a frequency of Love: for others, **Guidance Power System.**

We grappled with revealing the five gears and hand signals at this time. As Azima and Tianna continued to dialogue, an awesome awareness emerged that the seed of the GPS Code was hinted at in what Tianna heard mystically: "Surrender, Each day, Step by step, You will be shown the way." We marveled that the daily discipline and two of the five gears were obvious in this quote. At this point, it was evident that it would not be in the highest and best interest of you, the reader, to get a sketchy look that could not be easily applied.

Yes, they are called gears for a greater reason that takes you beyond steps. The gears appear simple yet are significantly more than they appear to be. If you desire a deeper understanding and fuller experience of this **GPS Code,** we are thrilled to take you to your next level. Please visit https://www.yourgpscode.com and enjoy the trip called evolution!

We can assure you that by setting your innate GPS your soul will be in the driver's seat of your vehicle. As with your car, this system will select your destination to the best solution to your problem, shifting you from self-sabotage to self--empowerment. In the words of Einstein, "When the solution is simple, God is answering."

One of the undisclosed gifts that Tianna received in the NDE is that the chatter of her "monkey mind" was silenced. Passed on through the GPS Code are the abilities to quiet your mind and a simple way to release your emotions so they are expressed rather than repressed or suppressed. Essentially, it's about shifting from reactive to responsive living for an extraordinary journey.

Feeling fulfilled at a level that defied her conscious mind, Tianna embraced that her NDE had given her the pieces for a sneak peek into the bigger picture of her life. As Azima listened to these profound revelations, she was awestruck and speechless. Tianna urged her shocked friend to be patient and compassionate with herself. Azima, in turn, connected with her heart to express her truth. The starting point for Azima was her affinity and guidance through music and sound healing.

As we discoursed and mused over the expansiveness of human consciousness, a memory came up for Azima. She remembered her Indian singing teacher once described Indian music as having no beginning and no end. While 22 notes are audible to the physical ear in Indian music, the intervals between these notes are microtonal. Her teacher had referred to entering worlds in these minute intervals, or vast states of consciousness, psychological and emotional, where the music took her. If we look at life as a vibration, the reality is that there is no beginning and no end. We both saw this as a metaphor for life.

We acknowledged that sound could be the bridge between form and invisible energy, between the manifest and the abstract. Azima's Indian music teacher further saw music as a path to self-realization. As we explored this possibility, the following quote came to mind, "In the beginning was the Word, and the Word was with God, and the Word was God" (John, Bible). Azima realized that if one sees God as vibration, as the frequency that breathed and continues to breathe us into existence, it makes sense that sound/music would be a pathway to our authentic Selves.

She took a quantum leap in her own evolution by realizing that God is beyond form, beyond masculine and feminine. An ecstatic Tianna chimed in, "Anyone that gets this understanding sets themselves free." At this point, Azima referred to a quote from her mentor in spirit and Sufi mystic, musician Hazrat Inayat Khan, "They have said that the soul entered the body through music. In private, they have said that the music itself was the soul."

Azima began her conscious review of how important music had been to her since childhood. It had been her gateway to her soul's guidance in so many ways. As Tianna pressed her for more information, what started to unravel was the story of Crohn's Disease and how Azima nearly died several times. Although Azima admitted that medicine helped her, she eventually began to be more frightened of the medicine than the disease itself. So she began looking for alternatives or complimentary modes of healing. This is when her spiritual journey began to expand, and the following poem emerged:

I woke

In burst of light

To see Love's perfection

A glimmer of eternity

In you

As the pain of Crohn's Disease deepened, so did the writing and the music. The turning point piece that Azima was hesitant to share was the Angel song in which she had first felt the palpable love of angels. At that time, she was not ready to share the song because it had intimacy and love to the likes she had never experienced. She didn't want to lose that visceral knowing:

Angels surround me, enfold me with love.

Hold me and fill my heart with light and love from above.

Their wings encircle me bringing their peace.

Comfort, protect me bringing their peace.

They're with me always, in this I rejoice.

They're with me always, in this I rejoice (Angel Love CD)

In retrospect, Azima realized that her physical sickness was a portal opening for her into higher dimensions. It wasn't until many years later that Azima recognized that Crohn's disease had suppressed emotions that had not been acknowledged and continued to eat away at her until she began to face them. To listen to her cells, her needs, was part of her journey. This listening took different forms. Music was one.

Because music is vibration, it has the ability to connect directly to the frequency of our emotions. It can release emotions of pain, fear, and anger and bring harmony and peace to one's cells. For Azima, playing an Indian string instrument, the tamboura, and often chanting with it, released pent--up tears. As she continued this prayer, she felt nourished by their vibration, so much so that the accumulation of these chants became a CD (Passages Through Light) for others to enjoy and imprint in cellular memory.

Is there a musical instrument you play, music you enjoy, or chants that evoke thoughts, emotions, or body sensations for you? What would they be? For Tianna, classical music, especially Pachabel, came to mind.

Sounds also affect us in different ways. Toning and humming are simple methods that you can access anytime you need. These can help you to get in tune with your body and emotions: centering and lowering blood pressure are also benefits. This particular exercise activates the brain and cleanses every fiber in the body and brain.

It is a basic humming exercise.

Sit in a relaxed position with your eyes closed.

Purse your lips as if making the sound, "shhhhh"

Hum loudly, creating a vibration, particularly toward the front of your face.

Hum a single pitch continuously.

Imagine you are a hollow reed filled with vibrations of humming.

At some point you will become just the listener; the humming will be happening by itself.

You can do this until you feel a shift.

Another powerful form of vibration is chanting. A Tibetan abbot once had talked to Azima about this. He described it as prayer in which the feeling of the chant, with repetition, brings the person to a vibrational level where the request has already been answered.

For Azima, music continues to be her pathway to her soul's voice and to setting her free. In the words of Hazrat Inayat Khan, "Music touches our innermost being and in that way produces new life, a life that gives exaltation to the whole being, raising it to that perfection in which lies the fulfillment of one's life."

These memories had Tianna and Azima sometimes laughing, more often amazed at the opposite directions that they have lived in life, into their soul's nature. Since she was a little girl, Tianna had a more energetic, mystical perception of life. Experiencing death through the eyes of an NDE even anchored Tianna more toward the mystical point of view. Azima, on the other hand, in a more physical human way, came close to death at least two to three times and felt only pain, with often little hope. This anchored her into the struggle of the mortal point of view. We agreed that the dance between the mystic and mortal perceptions embraces the totality of life.

We trust that we have imparted wisdom from our extraordinary journey to empower the "extra" in your journey. Our message is that as we each awaken to who we truly are as infinite beings of Light and Love, we are here to live fully and leave a lasting legacy. We raise our consciousness by opening our minds and joining in the union of our hearts. This opens the gateway to the alchemy of personal and planetary transformation that is the ripple effect of awakening and an extraordinary journey for all! The words of Lao Tzu exemplify it best:

"If you want to awaken all of humanity then awaken all of yourself. If you want to eliminate the suffering in the world, then eliminate all that is dark and negative in yourself. Truly, the greatest gift you have to give is that of your own transformation."

***

To contact Dr. Tianna:

Dr. Tianna and Mary Azima (who recently passed into spirit) are deans: https:www.AwakeningAwarenessAcademy.com

Together we wrote our chapter, and although only Tianna's contact info is presented, Mary Azima is featured on the Academy page and transition tribute page: www.fearlessdying.com

Websites with gift: https://www.drtianna.com and https://www.shiftandgrowrich.com

Phone: 914-205-4969

Email: info@drtianna360.com

FB personal: https://facebook.com/tianna.conte.77

FB business: https://facebook.com/gpscode

FB group: https://www.facebook.com/groups/spiritualitymadepractical

Peggy Sealfon

Peggy Sealfon has a passion and talent for guiding others towards greater health, productivity, success, and happiness. With a background steeped in eastern and western traditions through extensive training with world masters, Peggy combines the wisdom of ancient teachings with breakthroughs in science and technology. As a personal development and lifestyle coach, Peggy is an international authority on personal transformation. Her "Mind Body Fitness for Life" programs empower individuals to master their mind and body, reverse aging, and reach their highest potential with ease.

An award-winning author, motivational speaker, entrepreneur, and podcaster, Peggy has been described as "crackling with vitality, intelligence and warmth." Her best-selling book, Escape from Anxiety—Supercharge Your Life with Powerful Strategies from A to Z, has helped countless individuals overcome stress, fears, and anxieties. She also published Embodying the Power of the Zero Stress Zone, the teachings of spiritual master Shri Amritji. Previously, she co-authored The Change: Insights into Self-Empowerment Book 9. Her first highly acclaimed work of fiction Awakening A Novel was published in 2020.

Peggy believes in the infinite human capacity for resilience, adaptability, and creativity to live more expansively. Her unwavering commitment to helping others has made her a beacon of inspiration and hope for those seeking to manifest a better world.

The Unfiltered Truth:

Discovering What Really Matters in Life

By Peggy Sealfon

If you believe life sucks. It does. It you believe life is glorious, it is. I have seen life from both sides now!

Over my decades of breathing earth's air, I have reinvented myself so many times that I have a lifetime of lessons to share. I've owned businesses, lavish homes, toured Europe alone at 19, had a fairytale wedding in New York City, rode motorcycles over 35,000 miles across North America, enjoyed international recognition and great successes.

On the flip side, I was bedridden for months with a fever of unidentified origin at age six. In my 20s, I became suicidal and was hospitalized with a nervous breakdown. I was diagnosed with a diastolic heart murmur, filed for bankruptcy in my 40s, got divorced. I've mourned the deaths of far too many loved ones, and yet here I am. Alive and well. I may be older, yet full of youthful spirit layered with experience. I've persisted through the polarities of life; the good and the bad. I'm grateful to be healthy, active, and full of vitality. So, what have I learned? What wisdom is worth unveiling?

As a youngster, I was timid and afraid of disappointing others, of saying or doing the wrong things. So, I quietly sat in the background making unconscious choices. My child within yearned for adventure and so I bumbled into many escapades, some were dangerous but that was the ecstasy, the rush of adrenaline. I was lucky to have survived.

One happened during a solo trip to Torremolinos on Spain's Costa del Sol. At the time, I was a journalist and seriously addicted to my Nikon camera. As I strolled along the main street of Calle San Miguel photographing storefronts and restaurants teeming with people bathed in the enchanted southern sunlight, two young Spaniards approached me. They were about my age and invited me to a most extraordinary site worthy of being photographed. Being from New York City, I was suspicious and momentarily hesitated, but they seemed kind and I did not want to miss seeing what locals valued.

My biggest mistake was getting into the back of the car with Roberto while Carlos drove on the road out of town. Suddenly I knew I was in trouble when Roberto began to molest me. I might be petite, but my feistiness and survival instinct kicked into high gear. To this day, I do not know how I managed to struggle out of a moving vehicle and, unhurt physically, I hiked my way back to town trembling and chastising myself for not being more cautious. I quickly realized when something sounds too good to be true, it may be.

A college boyfriend once told me: "If you are afraid to take risks, you will miss much of life." I took the concept to extremes. In fact, that became a crazy story of betrayal. We were only 20 when Stephen and I began dating as we attended New York University in Greenwich Village. He was an only child living with his widowed mother. He was smart, handsome but extremely possessive. We had been together for almost a year when I realized I needed to break free from his overly needy clutches.

When I tried to stop seeing him, he desperately confided that he had a brain tumor and was given only six months to live. He swore secrecy so no one would accidentally inform his mom, or it could destroy her. I was held hostage by this new development and felt compelled to hold Stephen's hand through the ordeal.

For months, I lived facing the death of someone I once cared about. He shared his fears, admitting that sometimes he just wanted to crash his car to be done. One day towards the end, he told me the doctors said he was in remission. Now he questioned what to do "about us." I walked away and never saw him again. The emotional toll on me was devastating. A year later when he was in grad school, he called to admit that the cancer story was a lie, that he was never sick. My response was to tell him that he was actually very sick. I hung up.

Not long after that, I developed mono (mononucleosis), a heart murmur and became suicidal leading to a total mental collapse. I suffered such intense upheaval that I became mentally and physically depleted. Chronic emotional stress suppresses the immune system. Clearly my internal turmoil was taking a mega toll on my body, my vessel for showing up in the world.

Stress is a killer. I had to find a better way, or I was going to die. I believe in synchronicity. An odd sequence of events aligned to bring me to a workshop featuring Yogi Amrit Desai (Shri Amritji). I was one of hundreds who came to learn from this world-renowned master, a pioneer of yoga in the west, founder of Kripalu and IAM Yoga. Dressed in traditional white kurta, Yogi Desai ("Gurudev") glided onto the stage. His teachings resonated deep within me creating a continual series of a-ha moments. He shared techniques that connected me to a sense of myself I had long forgotten. My stress, anxiety and fractured energies transformed into feelings of calmness, even happiness. I surrendered. Ultimately, I became a disciple. I went on to certify in both Amrit Yoga Nidra, a powerfully restorative "yogic sleep," and Amrit IAM Yoga; and subsequently Gurudev trained me in Quantum Breath Meditation.

As a writer and former journalist, I began collaborating with the master on a book about his transformational teachings which became Embodying the Power of the Zero Stress Zone. In the process I was immersed in his unique approach passed down through his lineage on how to enter the present moment through a shift from thinking and doing to feeling and being. I developed inner skills and discovered a profound connection to the divine source. This became a fundamental understanding to successfully manage the high intensity chaos of life. But I needed more. The spiritual practice created an effortlessness that seemed surreal. What was happening psychologically and in my biology?

So, I explored western practices and trained in everything from functional medicine and nutrition to neurolinguistic programming, neurosciences, and even esoteric energy healing. I could not stop.

Ultimately, what I realized is that everything works in an integrated way that opens you to unlimited possibilities. And what is most effective is what you believe works for you and aligns with your values and lifestyle. Life is about choices.

My intention is to be the best version of myself to continue guiding others in connecting to their source and supercharging their lives by cultivating mind body fitness for life! Life is a flow, a continuous unfolding. Experiences do not stop happening. Some are good, some horrific.

One downfall for me came in the year 2020 which was awful for many when a pandemic swept across the world. So, to support clients who I could no longer coach in person, I created "Mindfulness Moments from the Paradise Coast," a series of short videos showing nature and meditation techniques, aimed at de-stressing, and calming the nervous system. But the project "accidentally" changed my life.

Strolling on a stretch of beach along the Gulf of Mexico, I noticed a beautiful snowy white egret atop a massive stack of boulders. Carefully I climbed to the summit and felt a bond with this beautiful creature as I shot stunning videos. However, as I turned to descend, my bare feet slipped on the damp surface. I plummeted to the bottom and, not wanting to break my video camera, I stopped my fall with my left arm. There was a sickening sound as I landed with a thud and felt sudden screaming pain.

I refused to go to the emergency room in the middle of Covid. But days later the throbbing was so intense I finally succumbed to getting an X-ray which revealed I had crushed the radial bone--a comminuted fracture--and needed surgery. I was terrified. I had never had surgery in my life. My world stopped. I was homebound in agony. Following surgery, I suffered intolerable pain from nerve damage. During the day, I was isolated and alone as Patrick, my life partner, continued working. I dropped out of life. I filled my time listening to healing music, reading, and meditating. And then it happened.

A fictional story floated across my mind like a news chyron scrolling the bottom of a television screen. What did it mean? To be honest, a lifelong dream has been to write fiction and miraculously it was materializing. At first, my titanium-plated arm made it difficult for my fingers to tap the computer keys. It hurt. But I persevered. I had no choice. I had to write what was unabashedly shooting out of me as if blasted from a cannon.

The storyline was unformed. I had a basic premise: a 45-year-old divorced woman has a dreadful motorcycle accident forcing her to reassess her life and question whether she's wasted her years living all wrong. That was it. Very raw. Each morning, with my hot cup of black coffee, I'd get in front of my standing desk, plug my fingers into my keyboard and uncover the next juicy twist or turn that would befall my characters. What pandemic? What political chaos? I escaped. I disappeared into the writing, lost in the download from source. I watched in gleeful amazement as I virtually traveled the world with my characters.

Out of trauma and pain, there was a silver lining, a remarkable gift in manifesting my first work of fiction. Awakening A Novel has received rave reviews and three national book awards. I share this not to impress you but to impress upon you that adversity can lead to breakthroughs. Often, it is during our most difficult moments that we are forced to dig deep and discover strengths we didn't know we had. It can be challenging to see any benefit in misfortune, but it is important to remember that there is always an opportunity hidden within. We cannot grow from our comfort zone.

In my case, I had to be patient and always question "what am I supposed to learn from this?" It is a question we can all ask ourselves when faced with hardship. Whether it is a personal loss, a debilitating illness, or a major setback, the key is to stay focused and positive. With persistence and resilience, we can overcome obstacles and emerge stronger and wiser.

One of my biggest lessons has been to accept my own human vulnerability, to live in harmony between inner conflicts of being tough or yielding, establishing balance between extremes. I recall my days of training in Tai Chi and how I could yield to a 300-pound man coming fully at me and mysteriously dissolve that power. Doing so without resistance gives way to an inner strength that allows the fight to slip past without disturbing a single hair. It feels supernatural. The secret sauce.

It is common to judge every experience as good or bad, positive or negative. I've shared many of my harrowing life-changing stories with you. But at the end of the day, they're just stories. They do not define me. Your stories do not define you. What they do is give you experiences that you can grow from, that are woven into the fabric of your life's tapestry, your journey.

I encourage you to nurture your curiosity. Mine is insatiable and I never stop learning. In fact, I recently started exploring a breakthrough technology that reverses aging by activating stem cells. It is affordable and non-invasive, and delivers phenomenal results allowing me, my family, friends, clients, and pets to have more energy, focus, and longer healthspans. The discovery delights my childlike enthusiasm and sparks appreciation for the ingenuity of the scientist who evolved this futuristic invention available today. (LiveYoungerToday.com)

If you've read this far, you are likely open to receiving the truths of life. From all my experiences and training, I humbly distill in eight vital steps the raw reality of how to access what truly matters. Here they are:

1. Take time for self-reflection. Be grateful for your strengths and accept your weaknesses. You are not lacking or missing anything. Value yourself and be confident and accepting of all that you are. The more you access your true self, the more you have to give to others. You cannot give to others what is not flowing through you.

2. Release judgments of bad or good. Everything that happens contributes to personal growth and takes you further on your evolutionary path. Honor your experiences and be aware of patterns that may not be serving your highest and best self. You have choices. You can suffer — from worries, stress and anxieties that are imbedded in everyday life — or grow from every moment.

3. Take time to renew and refuel yourself. Eat healthfully. Consume organic produce rich in vitamins, fiber and minerals and feel the nourishment and fortification that optimize performance and health. Get quality sleep. Exercise. Appreciate earth's bounty. Saunter in nature and be awed by the magnificence of sunrises and sunsets. Experience the tingling of energetic vibrations in body, mind, heart, and soul.

4. Take brief respites from your endless list of tasks and focus on reducing stress and anxiety. Drop into stillness. The spacious silence is a profound place to reawaken your intuition, creativity, and life force. Meditative breaks can help you develop inner calmness and shift from survive to thrive. Instead of reacting to a jumble of emotions, find inner peace. Even in the face of disturbances —

irritating traffic, an annoying boss, a cantankerous child, an illness — release all struggles and relax with what is. Remember, you cannot change others or circumstances, you can only control your response to them. (If you have no idea how to meditate or want a quick and efficient "time out," download and use my free audio at 3MinutestoDestress.com)

5. Tap into your power center. Rather than fretting about playing life's roles perfectly — whether you're striving to be the ultimate spouse, parent, sibling, child, friend, employer, or employee — focus on being a compassionate and giving person. Practice unconditional love and open the floodgates to bathe yourself and everyone around you in an ocean of tranquility.

6. Don't defer happiness to the future when you expect external elements to be favorable. You are not your possessions, bank account, wardrobe or even your thoughts. You are an infinite being full of light, ingenuity, and possibilities. Uncover the place of inner contentment today. It's there. If you don't feel it, you're too busy. Slow down and simplify.

7. Enjoy modest tasks, the chores of everyday. They sustain the present and are the pearls. Don't look back and regret that you were too distracted to appreciate your first job, the early years of marriage, your toddlers. Be totally engaged in the moments of your life. Take time for hugs and kisses. Feel the warmth of running water as you do dishes. Revel in the clean fragrance of freshly laundered towels as you fold them. Enjoy the accomplishment of finishing a work assignment even if it pushed you to your edge.

8. Surrender to divine energy, a universal force. Life's magic happens when you bring body and mind into an ecstatically integrated state of being where you flow effortlessly in the light of consciousness filled with abundant gratitude and joy.

The most significant piece of advice I can offer is to give yourself permission to be you. As playwright Oscar Wilde once quipped "Be yourself. Everyone else is taken." Discover your authentic self and live fearlessly. Breathe deeply, dance wildly, sing to the sparrows and indulge as often as possible in hilarious laughter. And practice, practice, practice. To achieve the results you want, develop daily habits that contribute to accessing what truly matters for you. By questioning your thoughts and discovering the beauty of the present moment, you reveal the expansiveness of your own mind and heart to live a life of deep fulfillment and unconditional love. From that blissful state of being, you'll believe you have found heaven on earth! And so, it is.

***

To contact Peggy:

Email: Peggy@PeggySealfon.com

Websites:

PeggySealfon.com

MindBodyFitnessForLife.com

LiveYoungerToday.com

Social Media:

Facebook: https://www.facebook.com/peggysealfon.personaldevelopmentcoach

LinkedIn: https://www.linkedin.com/in/peggysealfon/

Instagram: https://www.instagram.com/peggysealfon/

Books:

Escape From Anxiety—Supercharge Your Life with Powerful Strategies from A to Z—EscapeFromAnxiety.com

Embodying the Power of the Zero Stress Zone

Awakening A Novel—AwakeningANovel.com

Renu Sethi

In 2007, I moved to the US from India with my 3 kids, shifted into a small apartment leaving behind a huge house, and faced a financial crunch in a new country with no social connections. Managing my kids along with some health issues that I had developed, I felt stuck. But being a survivor, a fighter, I never gave up. I figured my way out with my positivity and patience.

Rituals of mindfulness, meditation, and reading scriptures was a part of me ever since I can remember. But now, I began to explore the teachings of Louise Hay and practiced them in my life. Eventually, I healed and got life back on track, acquiring immense wisdom and realization in the process.

On mastering the personalized mantra meditation practice that I learned at Chopra Centre, I experienced psychological and physical improvements in me. I felt my energy and vitality revive, and I was brimming forth with happiness. I started to truly enjoy life.

I realized what helped me and my family could benefit many others, and I took the first step towards healing others, and the results have been magical.

With further study and certification as Chopra Health Instructor, I now help my clients achieve a body, mind, soul balance and enable healing holistically.

Change Beautiful Experience

By Renu Sethi

Change: Try not to resist the changes that come your way. Instead, let life live through you. And do not worry that your life is turning upside down. How do you know that the side you are used to is better than the one to come?

My name is Renu Sethi. I am here to share my journey. I was born into a conservative family in India and was the fifth child in a big family. As the youngest, I was always asked to listen and was often silenced. Despite this, I worked hard in school and was awarded certificates and leadership qualities.

My life changed drastically when I got married at a young age. It was an arranged marriage, which meant I needed to make a lot of compromises and adjust with The Man whom I didn't know. In India, marriage is not only between two people but a whole family. They expect too many things from the new bride, although I was unaware of their nature and expectation, so I started adjusting, making compromises, and trying to fit in a new atmosphere which was challenging but still not bad. I started enjoying my married life. I was lucky to be blessed with three children. First, one daughter, then twins, a boy and a girl. I got busy raising them. I also joined the family business, and we were doing quite well. Nothing seemed to stand in our way, whether it was family life or business.

Then out of nowhere, we got a letter from the U.S. embassy saying that our immigration papers were ready and we had been granted green cards. I eventually moved to the U.S. with my three kids on April 12, 2007. It was another big transition I had to make. This time I was in a place I'd never been with a new system and culture. Unfortunately, my husband did not move with us due to business commitments. When we landed, our new journey started—new people, new environment, not aware of anything. With three kids, our finances were also very tight.

Adjusting to the customs and culture in a new country can be another obstacle. I hadn't done any research before coming. It was very stressful and challenging but try to understand the hurdles we faced during that transition. We joined the Indian community to get help adjusting. The children were not at all happy. It was overwhelming for them and me.

There is difficulty in holding onto the past while also forgoing a new future. We come from somewhere, and, like the root of a plant, something ties us to a certain place and certain memories. Coming from thousands of miles away has made it difficult to bridge the gap between my old home and my new one, and not knowing what lies ahead has made it even harder.

 I find myself getting frustrated with the situation and feeling a sense of loneliness because I know that the life I left behind is not quite the same as the one I'm living now. Even though I have created a new life, I still miss my former home.

In my mind, it is always in the past not wanting to change at all kinds of stages of inertia. Where I was resisting change and clinging to the familiar, but it was not working anymore; I was trapped in a cycle that hindered my personal growth. I was fearful, miserable, and frustrated. It's like my life journey had stopped at one point. During this period, my daughter took me to yoga class. There was a mirror all over. While doing yoga, I saw myself in the mirror, And I felt the mirror was saying that the color in my face was not good. I wasn't looking well, very sad, and had no hope for life. Fearful, frustrated, resistant to change, and always living in the past, I felt ignored, unlovable, and lonely. The uncertainty of what lies ahead can often weigh heavy on the heart.

I was not at all gentle with myself. At this point, I decided no more looking back. I needed to embrace and accept the challenges and move forward. Isolation became my friend, and I started enjoying it.

I want to talk about my journey to spiritual enlightenment. Ever since I was a child, I have been drawn to spirituality and seeking a deeper understanding of life mysteries. Over time, I decided to make a more conscious effort to explore and understand the power of spirituality in my life.

So, I have been attending various workshops with spiritual teachers worldwide. These workshops allowed me to dig deep into the root of my spirituality and explore new ways of connecting with my inner self. I also found myself attending spiritual talks and lectures by influential spiritual leaders. These events left a big impact on my transitional period.

I began exploring spiritual growth and moved forward to adopt a new philosophy of life. I started participating in workshops, joining meditation groups, and living a holistic lifestyle.

There are many ways to change the spiritual approach. Changing your habits, for one. Routines will not help your transformation. The main motivator is changing your thoughts which can transform your life. The rest of my journey depended on this.

Change. There are physical and mental approaches to change. The spiritual approach understands all areas eventually equally transform. Holistic healing includes body, mind, and spirit. I started with the mental approach and attended a workshop engaged in meditation and yoga. We have to start cleaning any area; the choice is yours. The main concern is to change and adopt new transformations.

What would you choose if you had ten seconds to live the rest of your life? Things will always become clearer when you ask questions. In such a paradigm of creating a life that works for you, there is no right or wrong way of doing it. The past is gone, and the future is uncertain. All we truly have is now. By embracing acceptance, we can liberate ourselves from expectations and attachments holding us back. Living in the present allows us to focus on the most important thing: our happiness and success. Being in the moment also allows us to take pleasure in the little things and to see each day as a unique opportunity. It teaches us to appreciate life's beauty, marvel at its complexity, and embrace whatever comes our way with gratitude. We must learn to enjoy the ride, face each new day with optimism and courage, and look forward with anticipation and excitement.

We cannot go back in time and undo mistakes, nor can we predict the future. We don't always have control over our circumstances; however, we can control our attitude and the choices we make. We all have different paths in life, but by living in the moment, we can enjoy what we have and strive for what we hope to achieve.

As I watch my two daughters grow, I am reminded of this message. I want them to lead a life of purpose and take each challenge as it comes. I want them to find joy in each day and not be weighed down by fear or regret. I want them to know that the journey never ends, but with an open heart and optimistic spirit, they can find success and peace along the way. Attitude is like a flat tire. You can't go anywhere until you change it. We need ACE-Attitude, Commitment, Effort.

Start changing your thoughts about yourself. Embrace the awkward and uncomfortable. I was sitting in autopilot mode, but now I am in the driver's seat. I took responsibility and took charge of my life. I started being truthful to myself, keeping promises, and trusting other people equally. When you learn to fully appreciate your inner being and soul rather than just the body you are placed in as a vessel in this life, then you truly free yourself from limiting thoughts and understand the power of your worth. This will allow you to live the life you think only exists in your wildest dreams.

First, accepting and embracing, then comes the wisdom about surrendering our own higher self and embracing who we truly and authentically are.

"Change your thoughts about yourself living a life that is real inside and outside. The only validation comes from inside."

I was feeling lonely and isolated, but now I think the quieter you become, the more you are able to hear. It's your road, and you are alone. Others may walk with you but not walk for you. You must take your own responsibility.

After the mental changes, I started working on all methods of physical changes. Will, imagination, faith, and reason are states of consciousness that directly act from within.

When making changes, we must be aware of any resistance. This could be in the form of ego, fear, stubbornness, anger, righteousness, or withdrawals. These are holding us back from making the changes we need to make.

Some changes look negative on the surface, but you will soon realize that space is being created in your life for something new to change - Eckhart Tolle.

Consciously create space in your life where your heart can rest, and your mind can receive respite. We can't always control the situation we find ourselves in or the outside emotions that come with them, but we can control our internal states. We can choose not to abandon ourselves to violent emotions, such as medication or food.

Realizing all of this can give us the courage we need to make a change. After all, achieving a different result in life is simply a decision away. You have the power to choose how you will think and behave. You don't need to be bound by the same thought patterns that have been limiting you thus far.

Do we give up our former self while adopting change and growing into a real self? It may be hard for an egg to turn into a bird, but it would be a jolly sight to see it learn to fly while remaining an egg. We are like eggs at present. And you cannot go on indefinitely being just an ordinary, decent egg. We must be hatched or go bad.

When the caterpillar thought the world was over, it became a magnificent butterfly. What if that change you're avoiding is the one that gives you wings? It takes courage to let go of the familiar and embrace the new, but that's the law of life. If nothing ever changed, there would be no such things as butterflies. Butterflies are God's proof that change is good.

Change gave me resilience, power, a sense of freedom, independence, and connection to others. Changing myself enhanced my communication skills as well as my thinking skills.

Start practicing mindfulness which anchors in the present moment. Mindfulness practice also has transformative power. I encourage you to respect your intuition and understand that discomfort can be navigated; it is only temporary and can be a creative opportunity. Navigating change results in personal growth. When we grow on a personal level, we begin to feel more passionate about life in general. Stop thinking people will work for you. Fight your own battles. This is your journey. You are the author of your journey.

Wayne Dyer says:

"In the universe, there is an unmeasurable and indescribable force, which those who live off the source call intention, and absolutely everything that exists in the entire cosmos is attached to intent by a

connecting link. Sorcerers are not only concerned with understanding and explaining that connecting link. But they are especially concerned with cleansing it of the numbing effects brought about by all of the concerns of living at ordinary levels of consciousness. Intention and perception of looking at things play a very important role in our life."

Bob Proctor says:

> *"If you change your point of view yourself, your entire world will begin to change; changing your perception can allow you to SEE and attract your desired outcome.*
>
> *If you're not as happy, healthy, and wealthy as you'd like to be, take a step back and look at your situation from a different perspective. Look beyond the reason you've come up with for why you can't change or get what you want until you see a way to improve your current circumstances. Do it now and prepare to rewrite your story. Remember, perception is reality.*
>
> *Always have an attitude of gratitude. In today's hectic world, cultivating an attitude of gratitude is key. Taking a moment to express appreciation for yourself and those around you can bring meaningful benefits to your life. Practice gratitude and become happier, more optimistic, and more resilient. Expressing gratitude benefits my health, and I become less stressed and succeed in my work life."*

Ultimately, I will say success should be fun and not a struggle. Success is a static feeling. When you embrace change with an open mind to all opportunities, you will prosper and gain experience. It really comes down to the fact that no matter where life takes you, you always have to be prepared for change and be ready to adapt and adjust when necessary. And even though the changes can be difficult, they are also incredibly exciting and rewarding if you approach them with the right attitude. That's what I've learned over my years of marriage and living in the United States. I am so glad I took the plunge and went on this amazing adventure.

Integrate affirmations, meditation, positive attitude, and journaling into your life journey. These tools helped me and can help you to be more mindful, increase your awareness, and keep you grounded in the present moment.

Affirmations are positive statements you can repeat to yourself to stay positive and focused. They help you build self-esteem and keep yourself on the right track. For example, you can say to yourself, "I am deserving of success." You can also use affirmations to set intentions for yourself, such as: "Today I will be kind to myself and to others."

Remember: don't wait for success to be thankful. Be thankful for the opportunity to become successful! With the right mindset, you can make the most of every situation and appreciate the journey that brought you here.

Mahatma Gandhi Says:

"More I change More I get abundance, and everything happens for a reason or can anything happen by chance. Change become with attention and intention."

In the end, I just want to say I am thankful for my beautiful journey. It's been filled with plenty of ups and downs, and I feel blessed for all of the experiences I've had. Although I still have a long way to go, I'm happy to be on this path of exploration and open to whatever new things come my way.

Life is special and should never be taken for granted. It's important to take advantage of all the opportunities that arise and make the most of them. I try to stay positive and keep my head up, no matter what I encounter. Happiness is a choice that should be actively pursued no matter what.

My journey has made me wiser and more appreciative of things. I've been more open to trying new things and making connections that I never considered before. I'm thankful for all those who have helped me along the way and the lessons they taught me.

Speaking of lessons, I have learned that life is too short to dwell on the past or worry about what the future holds. Living in the present is key. Each day has the potential to bring something new, so always remain alert. Even when things don't turn out the way you wanted, recognize that it was just a learning experience.

I urge everyone to stay healthy, happy, and filled with joy. Don't let anything hold you back from living your best life. Life is a beautiful journey, and it's up to us to make the most of it.

Thank you for reading! I hope my words of wisdom help you to continue on your journey with positivity and eagerness.

Today I am feeling fully blessed to have such a significant transformation in my life. When I see people who are suffering and reluctant to change, I want to help them and encourage them to see the positive side.

***

To contact Renu:

Renusethi.com

FB & Insta

Renusethi.official

Email

Connect@ renusethi.com

Afterword

Life is always a series of transitions… people, places and things that shape who we are as individuals. Often, you never know that the next catalyst for change is around the corner.

Jim Britt and Jim Lutes have spent decades influencing individuals to blossom into the best version of themselves.

Allow all you have read in this book to create introspection and redirection if required. It's your journey to craft.

The Change is a series. A global movement. Watch for future releases and add them to your collection. If you know of anyone who would like to be considered as a co-author for a future book, have them email our offices at support@jimbritt.com.

The individual and combined works of Jim Britt and Jim Lutes have filled seminar rooms to maximum capacity and created a worldwide demand.

The blessings go both ways as Jim and Jim are always willing students of life. Out of demand for life-changing programs and events, Jim and Jim conduct seminars worldwide.

To Schedule Jim Britt or Jim Lutes as your featured speaker at your next convention or special event, email Jim Britt at: support@jimbritt.com or Jim Lutes at: mindpowerpro@yahoo.com

For more info on Jim & Jim visit: www.LutesInternational.com or www.JimBritt.com

For information on Jim Britt's online coaching course Cracking the Rich Code: http://CrackingTheRichCode.com

Master your moment as they become hours that become days.

Do something remarkable today! Your legacy awaits.

Blessings,

Jim Britt and Jim Lutes